# Tales from the Atlanta Falcons Sideline

## MATT WINKELJOHN

www.SportsPublishingLLC.com

ISBN: 1-58261-980-8

Publishers: Peter L. Bannon and Joseph J. Bannon Sr.
Senior managing editor: Susan M. Moyer
Acquisitions editor: John Humenik
Developmental editor: Travis W. Moran
Art director: K. Jeffrey Higgerson
Dust jacket design: Joseph Brumleve
Project manager: Jim Henehan
Imaging: Dustin Hubbart, Heidi Norsen and Kenneth O'Brien
Photo editor: Erin Linden-Levy
Vice president of sales and marketing: Kevin King
Media and promotions managers: Jonathan Patterson (regional),
    Randy Fouts (national), Maurey Williamson (print)

Printed in the United States of America

Sports Publishing L.L.C.
804 North Neil Street
Champaign, IL 61820

Phone: 1-877-424-2665
Fax: 217-363-2073
www.SportsPublishingLLC.com

*With good cause I doubt that all things are possible, yet I know as well that many difficult tasks are more plausible than first thought. It takes trying. I want my children—Patrick, Tori, and Roni—to know these things.*

*This book, my first, wasn't easy. At times, it seemed the target was 48 million words instead of 48,000.*

*Now that it's in your hands instead of in my head—or rather the heads of former players and coaches and on countless pages of research materials—I realize it wasn't that tough. It took time, patience, thought, and a willingness to change some plans on the fly, to adapt. Mostly, it took persistence.*

*Most people have these skills and traits, many of us in greater abundance than we acknowledge even to our inner selves, at least until being tapped.*

*Kids, believe you can, but beware the possibility that you can't. Use the prospect of one to avoid the other. Fear not failure, for it will find you from time to time. Instead, try, and I mean try hard. Tap yourself and grow from your shortcomings while knowing there will be some pain.*

*Earnest effort is the greatest endeavor you can attempt, and quite a pain reliever.*

*I love you to the moon … make that infinity … and back. Let me see you beat that.*

*M.W.*

*P.S. Grandma, I know you can see this from up there. I told you that I would.*

# CONTENTS

# ACKNOWLEDGMENTS

For the effort since 1965 of thousands of players, dozens and dozens of coaches and team officials, I'm thankful.

They have great stories, tales of the trials and tribulations not only of a football team, but of the undertaking of difficult tasks. Thank you for giving me something to chronicle. Competition is most noble, and writing about it—and its related tales—is a joy, a privilege even.

This book would not exist if Sports Publishing LLC didn't ask. For that, I'm thankful.

Records kept by the team were invaluable. A lion's share of material in these pages first saw light of day in *The Atlanta Journal* or *The Atlanta Constitution,* which were once competitors in the news world, or in *The Atlanta Journal-Constitution* once the papers joined forces.

I'm doubly thankful to the *AJC* for allowing me to undertake this project.

Other papers were great resources, as was former center Jeff Van Note, who should have been in the team's first Ring of Honor ceremony in 2004. Big Bob Whitfield was a riot, as usual, and we should all be so lucky as to be infected by like that passion of Super Fan Joe Curtis.

Of the many keepers of team records, Frank Kleha was helpful, and photographer Jimmy Cribb, an expert, was a rock.

Thank you all.

CHAPTER ONE

# All but the
# Biggest Mountain

B ack in the day, Dan Reeves was nimble as can be, strong
and graceful in his movements, an excellent athlete who
pushed his high school football, basketball, and baseball teams
from tiny Americus, Georgia, to statewide prominence in the
early 1960s. That didn't mean he could dance in the late 1990s.
He tried, though, after the biggest win in Atlanta Falcons history.

Five weeks removed from quadruple bypass heart surgery,
the Falcons coach on January 17, 1999, stood on a temporary
stage amid a strange humming sound in the Metrodome as
stunned Vikings fans fled the building as if it were ablaze.
There, Reeves set his surgically ravaged knees in motion, not so
much in conjunction with his awkwardly flapping arms, but
rather in a series of poorly coordinated semi-coincidental movements.

Reeves's version of the "Dirty Bird," dance—made popular by players in the best season in franchise history—was ugly to the naked eye. But it sure was pretty to Falcons fans, the symbolic cherry on top after his team rallied to upset the Vikings 30-27 in the NFC Championship Game.

Minnesota had been 16-1, was the highest scoring team in NFL history, and had a kicker who'd been perfect all season.

Yet the Vikings left the Metrodome hangdogs after their offense all but went to sleep once they forged a 20-7 second-quarter lead. The lasting memories for Minnesota fans were a failed 38-yard field-goal try by Gary Anderson and a 38-yarder by Atlanta's Morten Andersen that was true in overtime.

The Falcons have never had back-to-back winning seasons. But on that amazing afternoon in January 1999, the Birds had scaled every NFL mountain but the last, and biggest, upon punching tickets to Super Bowl XXXIII.

So the coach, running back Jamal Anderson, and cornerback Ray Buchanan danced.

"I'm opposed to all that stuff," Reeves said later, "but I've seen how good the 'Dirty Bird' has been for the city of Atlanta. There were guys standing on tractors at the airport doing it when we got home. There's no question it's turned this town around."

The city of Atlanta wasn't in such good shape early that afternoon because the Falcons were in big trouble.

Minnesota quarterback Randall Cunningham and wide receivers Cris Carter and Randy Moss were having their way with the visitors. The Vikings were 9-0 at home, beating opponents by an average of 25.6 points in the Metrodome that season, and Cunningham completed 11 of his first 12 passes for 114 yards and a touchdown.

The Vikings rolled to a 20-7 lead before getting a little too cocky.

A couple minutes before halftime, they faced third and 10 from their 18-yard line. Rather than run the clock, Cunningham dropped back to pass, and Falcons right end

Chuck Smith blew past Pro Bowl tackle Todd Steussie and knocked the ball out of Cunningham's hand. Defensive tackle Travis Hall recovered the fumble at the 14.

One play later, Chris Chandler hit wide receiver and Atlanta native Terance Mathis for a 14-yard touchdown, pulling the Falcons within 20-14 with 59 seconds left in the half.

"They were going for the knockout punch," Smith said.

Cunningham completed just 18 of his final 36 passes as Atlanta's pass rush grew stronger as the game wore on, even though the Vikings had three Pro Bowl offensive linemen.

After Anderson missed a 38-yard field goal that would've given Minnesota a 30-20 lead with 2:07 left in regulation, the Falcons took over at their 29-yard line needing a touchdown to force overtime. Fate seemed to be on Atlanta's side now; it was Anderson's only miss of the season.

Five plays later, Chandler's pass was almost intercepted by Minnesota safety Robert Griffith in the end zone. His composure, however, never ebbed. Soon the game was tied when Chandler and Mathis hooked up again on a 16-yarder with 49 seconds left.

"It was a do-or-die thing," Chandler said. "It was all or nothing. In a way, it makes it easier, because you know you have to score a touchdown. You don't have to worry about it being third or fourth down, you've just got to make the plays. You get so wrapped up in the game that you don't actually think about what is happening."

It was so loud in the Metrodome that afternoon that the Falcons used a silent snap count on every play. Yet they didn't have a single false start on any of their 75 snaps. The Vikings, on the other hand, were called for encroachment five times.

"Chris would just give me a little nudge, and we'd go from there," center Robbie Tobeck told *The Atlanta Journal-Constitution*. "They were trying to time it all day, but they couldn't. Eventually, they just gave up."

# GOOD AS GOLD

A ndersen's goal to become the NFL's all-time leading scorer continued through the 2004 season (when he kicked for the Vikings), when Gary Anderson came out of retirement yet again to stay just ahead of the former Danish soccer star.

On that memorable day back in 1999, he was as confident as ever before winning his personal duel.

Back in Atlanta, confidence was tougher to find.

Falcons fans at James Dawson's house in south DeKalb County stood in a semicircle around a table littered with chicken bones, beer cans, and pizza crusts. Arlene Dawson sat next to the television, where she couldn't see the screen. She hunched her shoulders and stuck her fingers in her ears. She knew she would be able to tell how the kick went by the men's reaction.

As the field goal flew through the goalposts, the men started jumping, shouting, hand-slapping, and cranking their hips. "Dirty Bird, Dirty Bird!" shouted Dawson, bumping his hip in the direction of the screen.

Bruce Jackson, a longtime fan, who watched at Jocks & Jills, a restaurant/pub at the CNN Center in downtown Atlanta, felt liberated in a way.

"This makes up for 1980," he told *The Atlanta Journal-Constitution,* referring to what up until that day had been the most notable playoff game in Falcons history, a loss to the Cowboys when Dallas quarterback Danny White threw two fourth-quarter interceptions to rally his team in old Atlanta-Fulton County Stadium.

"The Falcons played not to lose against the Cowboys and wound up getting beat. This has been a long time coming. The Falcons played to win against Minnesota, and they're going to Miami."

Indeed, shortly after the 26th game-winning kick of Andersen's career, which came with 3:08 left in overtime, he ran from the field, arms aloft. The man was happy, and why not? He'd negotiated into his contract a clause that called for a bonus

*Falcons kicker Morten Andersen (5) earned himself an extra $300,000 with a game-winning 38-yard field goal in the NFC Championship Game.*

of $300,000 if he kicked the winning field goal in the conference championship game.

"It was automatic, man," he said after the game. "Right down the middle, baby. It's all destiny."

## THE HOMECOMING DANCE

Late the night after the game, a huge crowd met the Falcons as they deboarded their charter flight at Hartsfield International Airport. Before they got off the plane, firetrucks sprayed water over the jet, an honor normally reserved for retiring pilots and the Braves when they have won division championships.

Big Dikembe Mutombo, the former center for the NBA's Atlanta Hawks, was in that group. "I did the 'Dirty Bird,'" he said. "I was so happy for them, I was dancing."

Atlanta fan Helen Lowe, who was also at the airport, said, "I feel like I'm in a dream. In a minute, I'm afraid I'm going to wake up, and it's not going to be real."

It was real, although even Reeves had a hard time believing. A day later, the coach was still amazed. After all, 15 months earlier, in his first season as the Falcons coach after stints with the Broncos and Giants, his team was 1-7. Suddenly he was on the way to his ninth Super Bowl as a player, assistant, or head coach.

"If ... somebody was writing a script for a movie, I don't think they could come up with one that's been like this season," said Reeves, whose team won six of the final eight games in 1997, and then 16 of 18 in 1998 (including playoff victories against San Francisco and Minnesota) on the way to the Super Bowl.

"From my standpoint, this is as excited as I've ever been to be in a Super Bowl, because it's certainly not something you would have thought was realistic when the season started. This team has been unbelievable."

# CHAPTER TWO

# Birth of the Birds

Middle-aged sports fans and longtime Atlantans might be surprised at some of the principle characters involved in bringing the NFL to the Peach State in 1966.

In the Southeast, most pro football fans in the mid-1960s followed the Redskins, because they were the team most typically on television. Geographically, the nearest pro team was the Cardinals of the NFL, and they were 467 miles away in St. Louis.

Unhappy with their stadium situation, Cardinals owners Bill and Charles Bidwill spoke during 1963 season of moving their football team to Atlanta, and they met with former mayor Ivan Allen Jr. to discuss the transition. St. Louis, however, committed to build a new stadium (Busch) and kept the team.

Multiple businessmen were interested in bringing pro football and/or baseball to Atlanta, and a maverick baseball man helped get the ball rolling.

When the opinion of former Kansas City Athletics owner Charles O. Finley was solicited (some would say offered without being sought), he visited and told some ambitious would-be team owners that the chances of bringing a pro sports team to Georgia would likely go nowhere without a sufficient stadium. He hinted that he might move his team, in fact, to Atlanta.

Within a little more than a year, Atlanta-Fulton County Stadium was built about a mile south of downtown, just east of I-75/I-85. It was managed by the Atlanta-Fulton County Recreation Authority, which was chaired by Coca-Cola president Arthur Montgomery. His role in bringing the Falcons to town would be significant.

Businessman Jim Clay and attorney William Schroder led a group that promoted several NFL exhibitions in baseball parks and high school stadiums, and NFL commissioner Pete Rozelle had suggested that Atlanta might get a team in 1967.

That schedule changed on June 7, 1965, when a group including J. Leonard Reinsch, the president of Cox Broadcasting, won from the upstart American Football League the franchise rights for the city of Atlanta for a reported $7.5 million.

This prickled Rozelle, and he traveled quickly to Atlanta to let his angst be known to then-governor Carl Sanders. Soon, Sanders had an idea, according to an old *Atlanta Magazine* article.

"I've got the man for you," Sanders said to Rozelle during a meeting in Atlanta in mid-June. Turning to a state trooper in the office, Sanders said, "Get Rankin Smith on the phone."

Sanders and Smith were friends, one previously having appointed the other to a post on the Georgia Game and Fish Commission.

"Rankin, what are you doing?" Sanders supposedly said on the phone. "Well, how'd you like to buy a football team? This

*Rankin Smith felt that every American male wanted to own a football team, and he made his own dream come true.*

fellow [Rozelle] has a plane to catch ... so get over here right away."

Within the hour, Sanders introduced Rozelle to Rankin McEachern Smith, executive vice president of The Life Insurance Company of Georgia that was founded by his grandfather. The 40-year-old outdoorsman later had a simple explanation for his new, somewhat forced, aspiration.

"Doesn't every adult male in America want to own his own football team?" said Smith, who described himself as a former reserve halfback at the [Jacksonvillle] Bolles School, where he was sent by his parents after stints as a student at North Fulton High and Atlanta's Marist School.

Rozelle did some homework to make sure of Smith's financial acumen, and on June 30, 1965, gave him a green light to set up an NFL team in town one year ahead of schedule so the team could begin play in 1966—if he could come up with a place to play games. That was not yet a lock.

Smith paid the NFL between $8 million and $9 million for the privilege, but the AFL and its commissioner, Joe Foss, were not giving up. They very much wanted a team in Atlanta.

As others lured baseball's Milwaukee franchise to Atlanta's new stadium, Montgomery—with whom Smith and others worked previously to get the stadium built—picked the new football tenant. After some behind-the-scenes politicking, Montgomery opted for the NFL, spurning the AFL.

Smith was tickled. "Atlanta has a lot of people from NFL cities—Cleveland, New York, Philadelphia, and Detroit," he said. "They have a great loyalty to the NFL, and they'll go out to see their old teams as well as the new Atlanta team."

As the AFL turned its sights on Miami (which got an AFL team in 1966), and New Orleans (which got an NFL team in 1967), Atlanta quickly was dumped feet-first into the business of speculation that accompanies sport. Reports quickly surfaced that the new stadium would get a roof.

"We can dome the stadium with a retractable fan-fold roof for about $1.5 million," Mayor Allen said. "The air-conditioning costs an additional $8 million, and there is considerable doubt in my mind that we need it. The weather is perfect in Atlanta 95 percent of the time, and the only thing we need is protection from rain."

Alas, Atlanta's stadium was not domed until 1992, when the Georgia Dome opened a couple miles to the north of Atlanta-Fulton County Stadium.

Meanwhile, Smith needed a name for his team, not to mention colors, a coach, and players.

## FALCONS IT IS

A slew of big names in the coaching profession came up as possibilities in Atlanta. Green Bay legend Vince Lombardi's contract was up; former Browns coach Paul Brown was mentioned; Arkansas coach, former Georgia Tech star, and Decatur native Frank Broyles was discussed, former Oklahoma coach Bud Wilkinson (who was in politics at the time) was bandied about.

Former Browns quarterback Otto Graham was said to be lobbying for the position, and Bears founder/coach George Halas threw the name of Tech coaching legend Bobby Dodd into the pot.

First, though, came the team's name.

Ernest Rogers of *The Atlanta Journal* suggested a few in print, including the Peaches or the Goobers, in honor of the state's peanut crop. He spurned the idea of the Knights for its connection with the Ku Klux Klan.

He also wrote, "The brown thrasher being our state bird one might consider calling our team the 'Thrashers,' but somehow or other, it doesn't seem to fit."

*Journal* sports editor Furman Bisher handicapped several possibilities in a column, including the Rebels (30 to 1 odds), the Smiths (14-1), the Rhetts (as in Rhett Butler of *Gone With the Wind* fame, 40-1), and the Baptists (90-1). Someone even suggested combining the mascots of Georgia and Tech and calling the new team the Yellow Dogs.

In the summer of 1965, there were two NFL exhibition games in Atlanta-Fulton County Stadium, the first featuring former University of Georgia star quarterback Fran Tarkenton and his Minnesota Vikings against the Pittsburgh Steelers on August 14. Tarkenton, in fact, threw the first incomplete pass, completed pass, and touchdown pass in the history of AFCS—all in that preseason game.

Two weeks later, the Steelers beat the Colts in another pre-season game in Atlanta, and afterward, Smith decreed that his team would be the Falcons.

The idea actually came from a contest soliciting input from fans, the winner being Julia Elliott of McDonough, Georgia, a school teacher in Griffin.

Judges for the contest were Bisher, *Constitution* sports editor Jesse Outlar, Dodd, Georgia coach Vince Dooley, and Phil Harrison, the public relations director for the WSB radio station, which co-sponsored the contest.

After winning four season tickets for coming up with the winning name, Elliott said, "The falcon is proud and dignified, with great courage and pride. It never drops its prey. It's deadly and has a great sporting tradition."

Smith also hired his first player personnel chief, former Detroit Lions scout Gene Cronin, who'd been a defensive end and linebacker before that with the Lions and Redskins. Former Lions assistant general manager Bud Erickson was hired as an executive assistant.

## SLIM PICKINGS FOR PLAYERS

Cronin got busy signing players, although there weren't many to sign. The NFL and AFL seasons were underway by this point, and the best football players were signed, of course, to contracts.

Still, it drew headlines when the first player to put his name to a Falcons contract, speedy wide receiver Bob Paremore, joined in early September. The former Florida A&M wideout had been cut by the Cardinals, and the Falcons quickly sent him to a minor league team in Lakeland, Florida, where he supposedly scored on an 84-yard play.

Another 16 players were signed that month, including tight end Taz Anderson, a former Tech starter, who'd been cut by St. Louis.

Smith let out word that the Falcons' uniforms would include some combination of red, black, white, and gold in honor of Georgia (whose primary colors are red and black) and Tech (black and gold). Soon, season tickets went on sale for $48, and almost every seat cost $6 individually.

The Falcons would get a big-time player months later, but not easily.

# CHAPTER THREE

# Falcons Get a Horn Up

As the Falcons in 2005 enter their 40th season in the football business, Tommy Nobis is one of two people who has been in the organization for all but one of its first 39 years. He signed on late in 1965, little more than one year before equipment man Horace Daniels, but only after resisting a call from outer space.

Landing the former University of Texas linebacker/offensive guard wasn't as simple as Smith and Cronin making Nobis the first overall pick of the NFL's college player draft. The AFL was again a meddler, as the two leagues held simultaneous drafts late in November 1965.

Nobis, a giant for a linebacker at six foot two and 233 pounds, had won nearly every award imaginable for the Longhorns, and shortly after the AFL's newest team, the Miami Dolphins, drafted Kentucky quarterback Rich Norton and

Illinois fullback Jim Grabowski as co-No. 1 picks (the first two picks being a reward for the expansion team), the AFL's Houston Oilers picked Nobis at No. 5.

Rugged to the bone, the San Antonio native's first comments to the Atlanta media were true to form. "I go where the ball goes," he said. "A man ought to have enough pride to play every game as hard as he can, wringing every bit of energy he has in him trying to win. That's the only thing that matters in football."

But which team would he go to?

For as raw as Nobis sometimes seemed—like when he said, "I hit 'em right in the goozle, high and hard. That way, they don't do anywhere but down."—he was no dummy. Texas coach Darrel Royal liked to remind people that his prize player was majoring in speech, and when the coach was asked the key to the 'backer's success, he said, "He ain't exactly eat up with a case of the stupid."

Given that Oilers owner Bud Adams vowed to break the bank in pursuit of Nobis, his future as a Falcon was in doubt.

Because the Falcons were an expansion team, the NFL granted them the first and last picks of each of the draft's first five rounds, and Atlanta's second first-rounder, quarterback Randy Johnson of Texas A&M, signed a contract the same day he was drafted. Nobis would take a while.

Unlike today—when drafted players have few options (other than playing for the team that picks them or not playing at all)—Nobis and some other drafted players had choices. Adams put on a hard sell, taking a page out of Nobis's book on how to approach things that matter—all-out.

Once the draft ended, the recruiting began.

"The value of Bud Adams's package was worth more than what Rankin could afford," Nobis recalled almost 40 years later. "He had some cattle in the offer, and he was in oil, Phillips Petroleum [which his father ran]."

*Widely recognized as one of the top NFL defenders of his era, Tommy Nobis lived up to expectation after the Falcons made him the first overall pick of the 1965 draft.*

## A CALL FROM SPACE

While the Falcons went immediately about signing other draft picks, Nobis scheduled a visit to Atlanta. He and Grabowski were about the only dual first-round picks who didn't sign quickly in one league or the other.

There was considerable commotion about the two record-setting players, driven in part by the fact that the AFL's No. 1 pick of the 1964 draft, Alabama quarterback Joe Namath, got a signing bonus of about $400,000, a whopping sum at the time, when the Jets tabbed him before everybody else.

While Nobis was in Atlanta, Adams said, "If he doesn't sign in Atlanta now, I think the Falcons have lost him. Nobis is at least a $400,000 ballplayer. We don't go by a budget out here, so there won't be any problem in signing him if he wants to play."

Adams in 1961 lost his No. 1 draft choice, tight end Mike Ditka, to the NFL's Bears, and he didn't want that to happen again. "The only reason we lost Ditka was we were a little lazy in the way we went about it."

Nobis, though, wasn't rushing his decision. He went from Atlanta to Houston, visited with Adams, and then returned to school. At one point, he told *The Atlanta Constitution*: "I'm so confused I don't know what I'm doing. I may have to just put aside the offers and decide where the hell I want to play football."

The Oilers kept recruiting from every angle—including space.

As astronaut Frank Borman orbited the earth in Gemini 7, he made his own sales pitch. Nobis didn't hear it directly—the message went to mission control at the NASA space center in Houston. But he sure heard of it.

"He radioed back that he certainly hoped that I would sign with the Oilers and not the Falcons," Nobis said. "Every time I think about that story, one of the neatest things that happened to me ... as I was walking from one class to another on campus that day, a co-ed came up to me and said, 'Aren't you Tommy

Nobis?' I said yes, and she said, 'I just saw a thing on the news and Borman said he hopes you'll play for Houston.'

"I thought she was kidding. I got back to my dorm, and turned on the radio or TV, I don't remember which, and it was true. He had to have a lot on his mind, and it was certain very meaningful."

## SHOW ME THE PRESTIGE

Nobis took nearly three weeks to make a decision. Adams was pushing hard.

"He offered me a couple future [gas station] sites, and I looked at those and I knew nothing about speculating and all that stuff," said Nobis, who's now the Falcons' vice president of corporate development. "Then he offered me, say, 100 head of longhorn cattle. I had a friend who was in cattle, and he went out and checked them out. They were all scrawny, and one might have a horn up and a horn down."

It didn't come down to money.

"I was very conservative and understood better what Mr. Smith had on the table," Nobis said. "Mr. Smith's deal was pretty straightforward. He was in insurance, and it did include some life insurance for me. On paper, Mr. Adams's deal was more valuable."

And on December 14, 1965, before the Falcons had a head coach, Nobis signed with Atlanta for a deal reported at the time to be worth $225,000.

"I got in the neighborhood of a couple hundred thousand dollars signing bonus, deferred over a number of years," Nobis said about eight months after another Falcons' first-round draft pick, DeAngelo Hall, received about $12 million in guaranteed money after being made the eighth overall pick of the 2004 draft.

"The contract, salary-wise, was a five-year deal, and the first year was $25,000. It accelerated every year for the next four years for $5,000 a year. I wanted to be a high school coach, and if I had done that, I'd have been making $6,000 to $8,000.

"So it wasn't the kind of money you could live the rest of your life on ... but it was good money at the time. Growing up, I was a big NFL fan, as many young men were. The NFL was the prestige. It had a little more prestige than the AFL, which had just been around a little while. Atlanta was a brand-new franchise, and everything about it was exciting."

## ADAMS CHANGES HIS TUNE

After Nobis signed with the Falcons, Adams said his highest offer had been worth about $250,000—not nearly as high as he'd indicated he was willing to go. The Oilers owner also sounded a siren of a different sort. The bidding war between the NFL and the fledgling AFL was bad for business.

He said the NFL was overpaying players because commissioner Pete Rozelle had strongly urged teams to do whatever necessary to land the top 30 players so the league could win a better television contract.

"This fighting over college talent is not good, not good for the owners or the players. Some athletes aren't thinking as much about football these days as they are their stockbrokers," Adams said then as teams in the combined leagues spent $7 million to sign college players.

"Either a [league] merger, or common draft is coming. I believe sincerely that within two or three years at the present rate salaries are going up what we'll have is almost every team [in both leagues] out of the black, and into the red."

A series of secret meetings in the spring of 1966 produced a June 8 announcement that the leagues would merge, although they kept separate schedules through 1969. Also, after the 1966 season, the AFL champion began annually meeting the NFL champion in a world championship game, which came to be known as the Super Bowl. In 1967 the leagues began holding a combined mutual draft.

Nobis, then, played a part, however small, in triggering the AFL-NFL merger.

# CHAPTER FOUR

# Vick 'N' the 'Stick

Michael Vick's lips were a little dry, so he did what he often does: he applied balm. Funny thing, though, he was in Candlestick Park, in a huddle, in the middle of the first game of his pro career when he pulled a tube of Chapstick out of his helmet before his very first play.

Say this of the four men who've been drafted No. 1 overall by the Falcons—including Nobis in '66, quarterback Steve Bartkowski in 1975, defensive end Aundray Bruce in 1988—they all had or have distinguishing characteristics.

In the case of Vick, the NFL's leadoff man in the 2001 draft, no Falcon ever fashioned a greater habit for dramatic flair. Yet for all his speed, howitzer-like arm strength, and endless reels of highlight plays, the former Virginia Tech quarterback has a steady, understated personality that is opposite to the pace of his play.

After making it to Super Bowl XXXIII following the 1998 season, the Falcons vanished into a dark cave, with records of 5-11 in 1999 and 4-12 in 2000. Then they packaged the No. 5 pick of the 2001 draft with return ace Tim Dwight, who was something of a fan favorite, and sent both (plus other draft choices) to the Chargers in exchange for the No. 1 pick in April 2001.

The opening pick still frightened San Diego officials after they bombed a few years earlier by making former Washington State quarterback Ryan Leaf the No. 2 overall pick.

So the Falcons nabbed Vick, who brought light into the darkness, although not by way of the spoken word. He was so painfully quiet as a rookie that reporters or even teammates in a huddle could barely hear him at times. That doesn't mean he was a nervous wreck. A rookie playing in his first NFL game, everybody watching to see what the draft's top pick will produce—and all the kid was concerned about was chapped lips.

Chris Chandler remained the starting quarterback that fall, but coach Dan Reeves made sure Vick received playing time in several games early, although Chandler complained that it hurt his rhythm.

Vick's first action came in the season opener at San Francisco. Fortunately, his teammates probably don't remember that he failed to complete any of four pass attempts. They may also forget that he ran for 25 yards on one of his first plays as a pro.

Running back Jamal Anderson, however, will never shake the memory of Vick trotting onto the field, taking his spot in the huddle while everyone waited for a television timeout to end, and then reaching up in his helmet.

"It's one of the most memorable moments I'll ever have in my entire life," said Anderson, whose grew up with a father who was a bodyguard for (among others) Muhammad Ali. "We were in our end zone because we were on the five-yard line, and he had Chapstick. He actually applied Chapstick in our end zone. We were all like, 'Oh my goodness.' So you know he couldn't

*Michael Vick, whom the Falcons made the No. 1 overall pick of the 2001 draft, busted out lip balm in the huddle during his first NFL game.*

have been nervous. He's one cool customer. I know he's a pretty boy, but damn."

Vick said he caught a ton of grief from teammates in practice the next week, but added, "I gotta have my Chapstick."

Wide receiver Terence Mathis said, "It was the funniest thing ever. I've never, ever seen anything like it. But it kind of broke the ice."

Atlanta got off to a 6-4 start that season, but ebbed horribly down the stretch, finishing 7-9 thanks to an atrocious running game. Anderson, who tore his left ACL three games into the 1999 season, tore the ACL in his right knee, ending his season after two-plus games. In his absence, running back Maurice Smith struggled with a bum knee, and Rodney Thomas wasn't much better. Smith led the Falcons with a paltry 760 rushing yards, averaging just 3.2 yards per carry. Thomas came in fourth with only 190 yards, trailing Vick (286, 9.3 ypc) and fullback Bob Christian, who ran for 284 on the season. The Falcons scored just nine rushing touchdowns all year.

Vick made many amazing plays as a rookie, going 1-1 as a starter. The win, though, came with an asterisk. In the Georgia Dome against the Dallas Cowboys when Chandler was injured, Vick was so nervous in his first start that Reeves eventually alternated him with third-string quarterback Doug Johnson on a play-by-play basis. The coach said the rookie was so jittery that he was rushing throws and running too often.

Blistex called Falcons officials in 2002—as the team was in the midst of an eight-game unbeaten streak—to try to convince the quarterback to switch to their product.

Mention of the lip balm came up occasionally in Vick's first few seasons, and it finally came out at Tampa on December 5, 2004.

In a 27-0 loss, when Vick was creamed by Bucs linebacker Derrick Brooks, the hit smashed Vick's hidden stash—he kept it tucked in his helmet—into his forehead, leaving a golf ball-sized knot. That sent him to the sideline holding his head.

The balm rolled onto the field, prompting Bucs defensive end Greg Spires to say, "Isn't that illegal?"

Apparently not.

Once former Falcons left tackle Bob Whitfield, ever a quipster, couldn't help himself when Vick pulled out his secret weapon in the huddle in his first season as a full-time starter.

He had a simple question for his quarterback: "You got any lotion in there?"

## CATCHING FIRE

Home Depot co-founder Arthur Blank bought the Falcons from the family of the late Rankin Smith Senior in February of 2002 for $545 million, the first of several notable changes in Atlanta.

Former Bucs running back Warrick Dunn was signed as a free agent within a month of Blank's purchase. Soon after, the team surprised almost all league observers by using a first-round draft choice on Michigan State running back T.J. Duckett

*Home Depot co-founder Arthur Blank paid $545 million for the Falcons in 2002 and quickly changed many things about the team.*

rather than a desperately needed wide receiver such as Florida State's Javon Walker or Hawaii's Ashley Lelie.

The Falcons' decision in that off season to cut Chandler was more surprising than the move to release Jamal Anderson after his second major knee injury in three seasons.

It meant that, at 22, Vick would become the NFL's youngest full-time starting quarterback since Drew Bledsoe in 1993.

He did not disappoint.

The season opener on September 8 fell on the hottest game day in Green Bay history. Several players were suffering from dehydration, and defensive end Patrick Kerney—the team's ultimate fitness specimen—fell asleep afterward with IVs in each arm.

Nonetheless, nobody was hotter than Vick.

He completed his first 10 passes, and Atlanta took a 21-13 halftime lead as he ran for a score and threw for another.

His 72 rushing yards overall (including runs of 18, 14, and 13 yards) set a record for Atlanta quarterbacks. He also triggered a last-minute drive to set up a 52-yard field goal by Jay Feely, forcing overtime, where Atlanta lost 37-34. In his first game as a full-time starter, Vick had set the franchise record for rushing yards—as a quarterback.

The Packers were impressed.

"Michael Vick has lived up to his expectations. He gets a Pro Bowl vote from me," said Green Bay coach Mike Sherman. "He did everything he had to do when he had to do it—with his feet, his arm, his capability."

An astonished Brett Favre had this to say: "I thought Michael played great. He can run around a lot better than I can. They would have carted me off if I'd have run that far."

# BITTER BEAR

Atlanta fell to 0-2 a week later, losing 14-13 to the Bears when Jay Feely missed a late 45-yard field goal attempt in the Georgia Dome. One of the happiest visitors was a former Falcon, Bears' backup quarterback Chris Chandler.

"I thought I'd still be playing for the Falcons, which means I was surprised that the change [owner] Arthur [Blank] made was me and not Dan [Reeves]," Chandler told *The Atlanta Journal-Constitution*. "But in my opinion, that's not going to be lasting much longer. I think Arthur is going to get this figured out pretty quickly when it comes to Dan."

A couple days after the game, Vick piped up, but not about Chandler.

He said that Bears defensive coordinator Greg Blache had instructed his defenders to go for his knees.

"After [a] play on the sideline, I heard that, and I turned around and said, 'My knees? Coach, what's that?' and he said, 'Your knees,'" Vick explained. "I said to a couple [Chicago] players, 'There's no need for that. We're all competitive, but that could be a career-ending injury.' Even though [Blache] said that stuff, they weren't going low; they just hit me hard."

Blache didn't deny the sideline conversation with Vick.

"Yeah, [Vick] made a comment to me at the time," said the Chicago assistant who once got in trouble with league officials for giving his players real bullets as a reward for big hits. "I said, 'Son, if you run, we're going to hit you.' He got his butt beat, and now he wants to make somebody look bad. Unbelievable."

Vick and Reeves later admitted that the quarterback need-ed to be more careful about what comments were delivered to the media—any furor about Blache's edict died quickly.

# EBB AND FLOW

In a victory over the Bengals a week later on ESPN, announc-er Joe Theisman said Vick's "athletic arrogance" was similar to that of NBA legend Michael Jordan and NHL super-stud

*Michael Vick's penchant for electric plays was immediately obvious when he became a full-time starter in 2002.*

Wayne Gretzky. Vick already had compiled 184 rushing yards, a 101.1 passer rating, four touchdown passes, and zero interceptions in 77 attempts in his first season at the controls.

Then, however, the Falcons lost at home to the Bucs—the eventual Super Bowl champions that season—as he completed just four of 12 passes,

They were 1-3, and, after Tampa Bay defensive end Simeon Rice knocked Vick out of the game spraining his right (non-throwing) shoulder, Atlanta headed to New Jersey a week later to face the Giants without their new superstar.

The Falcons had a new flame, but Reeves's feet were being held to the fire—he had a shaky record of 17-35 since his team played in Super Bowl XXXIII.

# CHAPTER FIVE

# Milking It Dry

Before the Falcons ever flew officially, they had to worry about other airborne creatures. Mosquitoes at the team's first training camp were like monsters, so meddlesome that the threat of malaria seemed real. However, they weren't the only bugs in the works for owner Rankin Smith and his new team—not by a long shot.

The Falcons' startup might seem nostalgic years after the fact. It was anything but warm and fuzzy as it was happening.

In reality, the NFL's newest franchise was more like a weigh station with players coming and going each week as the first training camp approached.

Some players wanted to play in Atlanta, like Bears linebacker and former Georgia Tech star Larry Morris, who told Chicago owner/coach George Halas the only way he was playing pro football in '66 was if he was traded to the Falcons.

Morris made his off-season home Decatur, just outside of
Atlanta, and was building quite a real estate business. Halas said
no.

Former Colts star defensive back Andy Nelson, who was
out of football in '65 while selling sporting goods in Baltimore,
made the drive south to try out. After all, he had six kids, saying, "My milk bill is $50 a month."

Others, like former Lions defensive end Sam Williams,
whom the Falcons chose in the expansion draft, wanted no part
of it. He didn't show up, and team officials considered him
retired.

Linebacker Tommy Nobis and quarterback Randy Johnson
were among 25 college players picked by the Falcons in their
first draft—in November 1965. Within months, 39-year-old
Norb Hecker, a former assistant under Green Bay icon Vince
Lombardi, was hired as head coach. He arranged a coaching
staff that included legendary former Los Angeles Rams receiver
Tom Fears.

The NFL also created for Atlanta the most liberal expansion draft in league history, and the Falcons plucked 42 veterans
from teams around the league, including former Packers running back Junior Coffey and former Colts receiver—and legendary roustabout Alex Hawkins.

Some 130 players showed up for the team's first training
camp, which was held at Blue Ridge Assembly, a YMCA-owned
camp in Black Mountain, North Carolina, about 15 miles west
of Asheville, and in the shadow of Mt. Mitchell, the highest
point east of the Mississippi River.

"No, the facilities certainly aren't ideal," Hecker told the
*Charlotte News.* "The boys have been very good about adjusting
to the situation, though. There are no gripes, and the spirit has
been very good."

That was bunk. There were plenty of gripes. Before camp
ended, some players probably wished they were in Vietnam.

Coffey's arrival was delayed by an airline strike, and he had
to drive from Oregon. He was lucky to be late. In his absence,
everybody was miserable. There was intense heat, lots of mos-

quitoes, crummy food, dirt paths, high grass, and potholes on the practice fields.

And showers?

"They just took an old storeroom and ran some pipe up the wall, and it just kind of ran out the door," explained Tommy Nobis. "If you didn't get in there early, you weren't going to get any hot water."

But there was booze, although it wasn't exactly easy to acquire. It took after-hours road trips to get it, which sure didn't stop some players.

Hecker wanted Hawkins, who'd spent seven years backing up Colts receivers Raymond Berry and Johnny Orr, to be a leader among players since he had experience on a championship team.

A story in the *Los Angeles Times* suggested that Hecker's idea died the night Hawkins rolled up at five in the morning on the back of a watermelon truck.

"Do you want to say anything in your behalf?" Hecker asked.

"Would you believe I was kidnapped?" Hawkins replied.

There was quite the collection of misfits and wannabes on that mountain.

"In the off season, all those guys had jobs. The average salary at that time was probably $10,000 to $12,000," Nobis said. "Most of it was pretty close to manual labor. We didn't have a lot of new cars in our parking lot."

So didn't last that long.

"We were there for over six weeks, and during that time of the season NFL players received only $10 per day. This training camp period for many a player, financially, did create some problems. With a weekly paycheck of only $70 (for six weeks), some of our players had a difficult time paying their family's bills.

"Running back, Ernie Wheelwright, who came from New York [in the expansion draft], he had a new Cadillac. One day, players and coaches watched as the county sherriff and a smoking wrecker came and took Wheelright's Caddy away—repossessed it."

He failed to talk the men into leaving his car, and later had to find a ride back to Atlanta.

Not even famed evangelist Billy Graham, who lived nearby and visited camp one day, could save these poor souls.

"There were no screens on the windows and the mosquitoes were as big as birds," said Al Thomy, a sportswriter who covered the team for *The Atlanta Constitution* from their inception to 1978. "We almost had the first NFL players' strike over the food. The hamburgers bounced off the floor. The players threatened to go on strike if they didn't improve the food."

Ah, the food—it wasn't good.

"Some players got food poisoning, they shut the kitchen down," Nobis said. "I was a guinea pig. Some had diarrhea. They were trying to figure out what it was. They sent me to the hospital, and had me crap in a pot or whatever it was to try to figure out what it was. We're getting ready for our first ever game, and I'm coming out of the hospital from dysentery. Black Mountain—it was pretty rough."

## A NEW GIZMO

Fitness was a hit-or-miss proposition in the NFL decades ago, and most players worked themselves into shape at training camp rather than working out almost year-round, as they do now.

The Falcons, though, had a new gizmo in that first camp— something of a prehistoric *Bow-flex*.

Players were working out on something called, the, "Exer-Genie," which was described as nothing more than a chopped-off flashlight with a hook at one end, and a pulley with a string through the other. The pulley was attached to a fixed post, and the user strained isometrically against whatever pressure was chosen on the weight dial.

The machine cost $23, and debuted a year earlier in the Packers' camp, where Hecker had first seen the contraption. The inventor, Gene Harrington, spent about a week with the Falcons, teaching them how to use it.

"We have figured that doing three sit-ups properly with the 'Exer-Genie' is equivalent to doing 180 normal ones," Harrington said. "We added 10 yards to Bart Starr's passing last year."

## ALMOST REAL GAMES

Once the preseason rolled around, the starting quarterback was Dennis Claridge, who had been plucked from the Packers in the expansion draft after backing up Green Bay's Bart Starr and Zeke Bratkowski.

Former Georgia Tech quarterback Billy Lothridge, who was gained in the expansion draft, was struggling at free safety. He would end up Atlanta's first punter.

Claridge, it turns out, was re-signed.

In the first preseason game, in Atlanta against Philadelphia, the Falcons lost 9-7 when a late 37-yard field goal try by Bob Jencks was foiled by a bad snap from Bob Whitlow, the backup center. He was in because the regular center, Frank Marchlewski, had a neck injury.

Atlanta then lost 20-10 at St. Louis, 14-7 to the Giants, and 42-3 to Cleveland, in Atlanta-Fulton County Stadium.

After that one, Browns coach Blanton Collier said, "I beg of you, Atlanta people … be charitable and be patient. It takes a long time to build a professional football team."

For the preseason finale—against the 49ers in Columbia, South Carolina—Hecker made rookie Randy Johnson, his starting quarterback.

The Falcons won 24-17.

It was a mirage.

## COMING AND GOING

As the roster was pared down, Nelson, the sporting goods salesman/defensive back, was released. Halas finally relented, and Bears linebacker Larry Morris was traded to the Falcons, where he'd spend just one season—he wasn't much of a factor.

Sam Williams, the holdout defensive end who'd played for the Lions, showed up finally. He helped, too, both on the field and in setting a tone.

"He was … an old Navy guy with tattoos," Nobis said. "His rookie year he was like 28. We got him when he was about 35. He was a rough, tough guy. He played defensive end in the mid-'60s with a single bar, and if they'd have let him play without a facemask, he'd have played without one. He'd push it way down like some of those kickers. There was not a game where he wouldn't come out with blood all over his face. He didn't get going until he got a little blood going."

Wheelwright made the cut. In fact, Atlanta *Daily World* sports editor Marlon Jackson wrote that Wheelwright, "is a swinging pianist, and will be co-starred with Gladys Knight and the Pips … at the Pink Pussycat."

## IT'S MAYHEM, ESPIONAGE, AND RANDY

That was the headline in the Constitution after the Falcons' first regular-season game.

The Rams rolled into town, unleashing the Fearsome Foursome—the vaunted pass-rushing quartet of Rosey Grier, Deacon Jones, Lamar Lundy and Merlin Olsen—on Johnson before a soldout crowd of 54,418 in Atlanta-Fulton County Stadium on September 11, 1966.

Los Angeles raced to 16-0 lead before the first score in Falcons history, a 53-yard pass from Johnson to former Clemson starting wide receiver Gary Barnes.

The Falcons made it close before losing 19-14.

Hecker and his staff were positive that they'd have beaten the Rams if Jencks, the kicker they cut four days earlier, hadn't gone straight to the Rams looking for a job. Los Angeles had arrived in Atlanta several days before the game, and Jencks went to their hotel. Hecker believed that he gave away secrets.

"They knew our plans, and kept calling our signals to confuse our guys all day," the head coach said.

George Allen, who made his debut as an NFL head coach that day on the Rams' sideline, tried to dismiss the suggestion that he used a spy.

"We didn't change a single thing," Allen said. "No, we didn't get their audibles or anything else from Jencks. But the Falcons knew all about us. They got two players [Joe Szezecko and Bob Sherlag] who had been with us all the way. There's nothing unusual about that."

Reached a couple days later by the *Constitution*, Jencks said, "I'm not surprised Hecker would say a thing like that," Jencks said. "I talked with the Rams, but only about a job. I was out of a job, and I went looking for one. It's as simple as that. I didn't give any information to anyone."

## BALL BEATS KICKER

After the Rams game, Grier told the late Jeff Denberg, a sportswriter at the time for *The State* of Columbia (SC): "This is no baloney. That's a helluva team. They would have murdered those other first-year teams. Dallas and Minnesota couldn't touch them for organization and talent."

It was just another mirage.

Atlanta was spunky a week later, losing 23-10 at Philadelphia to continue what became a nine-game losing streak.

That game featured one of the Falcons' indelible, infamous moments. Kicker Wade Traynham botched the opening kickoff, barely grazing it.

"Just as I started to meet the ball, I noticed the Eagles dropping back and bunching around the receiver," he said. "I decided to change the direction of my kick, and when I cut across the ball, I didn't get enough of it."

No, it got him. Traynham strained a thigh muscle, and guard Lou Kirouac took over as the kicker. He connected on nine of 18 field goals and 19 of 24 PATs the rest of the season, which Traynham missed.

# CHAPTER SIX

# Two Kings Under One Roof

Although Home Depot co-founders Arthur Blank and Bernie Marcus were notorious for giving middle managers great leeway to run their own stores, that wasn't exactly what Blank had in mind when he bought the Falcons on February 2, 2002. It didn't take long for him to figure out exactly whom he wanted to run his new show.

"Right after I bought the club, I spent a lot of time talking to people, and I knew that I was not any great professional in a football sense," Blank told the *Journal-Constitution*. "I thought we had a reasonable cast, but I made a decision that I didn't want to have a team that was driven by a single person.

"I was not comfortable in that situation. It's not the way I work best. I like to get everybody's thoughts, everybody's ideas, get the best of everybody's thinking and move forward. I like a very open environment, and I didn't necessarily think we had that at the Falcons."

There were examples of head coaches who'd succeeded over time while holding considerable—if not complete—sway over player personnel: most notably Bill Belichick in New England, Bill Cowher in Pittsburgh, and Andy Reid in Philadelphia.

Essentially, Coach Dan Reeves had been his own general manager. Harold Richardson held that position (in title) from 1998 until Blank fired him in the spring of 2002. Blank, though, had a different front office structure in mind.

"I made a decision when I bought the team that I wanted a strong GM, and I also could not find any example in the NFL despite many attempts of coaches taking on the GM role ... where the job could be done," he said. "I thought the capacity was overwhelming. To be honest, we spoke to a lot of people at 280 Park Avenue [the NFL office], and people around the league, and the name McKay came up a lot."

That would be Tampa Bay Bucs general manager Rich McKay.

"He was considered to be the premier, if not one of the best, in the league. We also chatted with [Baltimore's] Ozzie Newsome, who still is considered to be one of the top GMs," said Blank.

As general manager of the Buccaneers, McKay and coach Tony Dungy built the Tampa Bay franchise into a perennial contender. Dungy was fired by Bucs owner Malcolm Glazer after the 2001 season—against McKay's counsel.

The ownership group also rejected McKay's recommendation to hire former Ravens and Redskins defensive coordinator Marvin Lewis. Suddenly, McKay was on the periphery in Tampa.

As Blank was buying the Falcons, the Glazers were negotiating with then-retired coach Bill Parcells to replace Dungy, and take the Bucs' GM title, too. "A search firm [hired by Blank] had called me ... to see what my status was going to be in the event Parcells was hired and made GM," McKay said.

Once Parcells backed out, McKay sought to hire Raiders coach Jon Gruden, but Oakland owner Al Davis set too high a price in exchange. Again, the Glazers got busy, setting up an

*Owner Arthur Blank and GM Rich McKay*

interview with 49ers coach Steve Mariucci. San Francisco would not grant permission for Mariucci to interview, however, until it was for both coach and GM. The Glazers agreed. McKay again was an island.

"When [the Bucs] went down the Mariucci path, I asked [the Glazers] for permission to talk to Atlanta," McKay said. "I spent about six hours with Arthur that day. I'd gotten an incredibly good feel for Arthur that day, and I had an idea of the way he envisioned setting up the franchise, which I liked. His commitment and his passion, he pretty much wears on his sleeve. He certainly gave the impression that he was in it for all the right reasons.

"He takes great pride in the city, the community, the state, and he views the Falcons as an important part of that. He just wants to make the whole thing better. He wants to win, but with some reality of what it takes. It was clear money was not going to be an issue."

But there would be an issue. On Valentine's Day, 2002, a Blank-McKay meeting led to nothing substantial, because soon the Glazers approached Gruden and Al Davis on their own, and worked out a deal. "Within days ... Jon Gruden was hired, and Jon was not hired as a GM, and not given a GM's authority," said McKay, who returned to Tampa Bay, and got a fat contract extension.

"It was during the Winter Olympics in Salt Lake City," Blank said. "I remember, gawdarn, it's early in the morning, and Rich called me and told me that despite our discussions, it was just something he couldn't do. It didn't make my day, but I understood."

Blank didn't hire a GM, not even after interviewing former Saints GM Randy Mueller, Seahawks official Mike Reinfeldt, Bucs assistant general manager Tim Ruskell and retired Packers official Ron Wolf.

He did hire former Redskins and Chargers GM Bobby Beathard out of retirement, partly on the advice of Falcons minority owner Joe Gibbs, the former Redskins coach who at the time was out of football, and making it big in NASCAR. Gibbs and Blank knew each other in part because Home Depot sponsored one of Gibbs's racecars. Beathard was named senior advisor.

"Joe Gibbs had talked about Bobby, and he had nothing but wonderful things to say about him and really felt like as a stop-gap measure, he would be terrific as a senior advisor, sort of pseudo-GM until I could sort all that out," Blank said.

"I also felt a lot of my focus initially had to be on the fans, and getting the Dome filled up, and we could continue to work on the football side of things with the staff we had, and see if Rich would eventually become available. I had no idea his relationship with Jon [Gruden] would become sour as it did."

After McKay, Gruden and the Bucs won the 2002 Super Bowl, they were unable to co-exist peacefully, or at least comfortably in 2003. Gruden kept making player personnel requests. "I felt like I was constantly in a position where I had to say no," said McKay.

Blank was keeping tabs, mindful of the stories surrounding his NFC South rival during the 2003 season, which was a disaster in Atlanta, where Michael Vick missed the first 11-plus games with a broken leg. The Falcons went 2-10 in those games.

"I started to read the same stuff you would read about how the relationship was not going well down there," Blank said. "I'd asked Bobby [Beathard] to extend another year, but I knew he didn't want to do it indefinitely. We really were just very fortuitous in terms of the timing.

"I give a tremendous amount of credit to the Glazers. The family understood that for whatever reason there was a rift between the coach and the general manager, and that Rich and his father [John, the Bucs' founding coach] had done a tremendous amount for the organization.

"They understood as well that Rich, who by nature is a very happy person, had turned into a guy who was not very happy, and went to work every day in an environment that he wasn't comfortable in, and didn't want to stay in."

McKay was hired on December 15, 2003, signing a six-year contract worth more than $12 million less than a week after Dan Reeves was fired. Some Atlanta sportswriters refer to Blank and McKay as Kings Arthur and Richard. "It's [Blank's] team, and his vision because he's the owner," McKay said. "It just happens to play right into the way we'd done it in Tampa, and the way I'd like to do it here. But the owner sets the tone."

In no time, McKay jumped into the coach hunt, joining meetings at Blank's house in the posh Atlanta enclave of

Buckhead, where Beathard spoke of a young coach who'd been on the San Diego staff while he was the Chargers' general manager roughly a decade earlier.

That would be San Francisco defensive coordinator Jim Mora—son of former Saints and Colts coach Jim Mora.

## BLING-BLING AND A BREAK

It would be hard to pick a stranger place than the Senior Bowl for new Falcons employees to break in, but that's where Mora, assistant general manager Tim Ruskell, and others debuted in January of 2004.

The annual college all-star game, always in Mobile, Alabama, is a favorite of NFL coaches and scouts for several reasons. Scouts love to watch practices, where they can see many of the players who'll be drafted a few months later and get an idea how they work and so forth. Recently fired coaches and front office employees tend to loiter, looking for work. Think of it as network central.

Imagine this setting: In the hotel that served as the league's command center that week, exhibitors were set up, showing the latest, greatest videotaping technology, etc. In the reception rooms, coaches, scouts, draft-eligible players, agents, and front office officials were all over the place—like bees on honey.

In one lobby, Jake Arians—son of long-time NFL assistant Bruce Arians, was selling cubic zirconia jewelry—*bling-bling*, or fake ice. A couple years earlier, Jay Feely edged out Arians in training camp for the Falcons' kicking job.

Former Falcons reserve running back Ron Rivers was working the room as an apprentice for Dallas-based agent Drew Pittman.

James Daniel—recently released as the Falcons' tight ends coach after Mora took the reins—and former Atlanta linebackers coach Billy Davis was there. So was Richardson, the former Falcons general manager whom Blank fired. He'd been out of the game for nearly two years and wanted back into the league. They were all in street clothes—the sign of NFL unemployment. Most coaches and team officials go out of their way to wear gear from their teams. Former Falcons assistants Rennie Simmons and Jack Burns, for example, wore Redskins hats and jackets; having been recently re-united with old—and new—Washington coach Joe Gibbs.

Across town, on one of the practice fields, with hands on hips in his standard pose, stood Wade Phillips, smiling in Chargers gear. A couple weeks earlier, Mora, McKay, and Blank fired Phillips as the Falcons' defensive coordinator after Atlanta finished dead last in the NFL in total defense and several other categories—chiefly because he insisted on sticking with his beloved 3-4 system even though he had better personnel to play a 4-3.

No matter. San Diego coach Marty Schottenheimer, whose staff was coaching one of the Senior Bowl squads, had hired him in no time. The Chargers, by the way, would go on to win the AFC West in 2004, and Phillips's 3-4 was a big reason why.

Anyway, after practice, Phillips said to an Atlanta writer, "So one of your new guys ain't too quick on his feet, huh?"

What?

"Ruskell."

Huh?

"The guy was working so hard at his new job he broke a leg. Jeez, I know more about your team than you do."

It was true.

Ruskell had been on the job only five days. Five weeks after escaping Tampa Bay, McKay had hired Ruskell—his right-hand-man in Florida.

And Ruskell broke a leg almost right off the bat.

Scouting players from the sidelines one practice, Ruskell was wiped out when former Alabama running back Shaud Williams careened out of bounds. Ruskell suffered a non-displaced fracture of the tibia below his right knee. Blank was bumped on the play, prompting him to embellish later.

"He saved my life," Blank said. "He left his feet diving."

Ruskell said, "I couldn't get out of the way."

*The Atlanta Journal-Constitution* had fun with this, printing a revised scouting report on the Falcons' newest employee:

*Reaction time: sloth-like; Quickness: none; Agility: statuesque; Durability: get serious; Intangibles: brave (or not so bright?), but shows little concept of how to land safely once hit.*

*Summary: Might be OK in a press box, but a disaster working the chains.*

At the 2005 Senior Bowl, the "Ruskell Rule" went into effect. Unless you're coaching a team, you have to watch practice from a distance.

## BLOWING BBQ

The Senior Bowl misery didn't end at the hospital for Ruskell. He and McKay have known each other more than 25 years, meeting as ball boys in the 1970s in Tampa Bay, where McKay's father, the late John McKay, was the Bucs' original coach. They were almost inseparable—so perhaps it was appropriate that they experienced their Falcons indoctrination together.

Few professional sports teams have endured more wretched moments than the Falcons, whether in the form of losing seasons (27 of the first 39), failed draft choices, blowout losses, ham-handed coaching changes, or whatever.

There's been some real wretching, too, and not just when Nobis and his teammates got food poisoning at that first training camp in 1966. McKay and Ruskell wretched at their first Senior Bowl with the Falcons. And they had company on their hands and knees, right up the ladder to owner Arthur Blank.

Ruskell was hobbling, yet still set a pace of sorts as the first of about half a dozen Falcons officials to get sick the night after the group dined at a local Bar-B-Q joint in Mobile.

More than a year later, McKay had a hard time recalling the story; he couldn't contain his laughter. Yeah, right. Once McKay gets going, he can *always* tell a story.

"His wife [Linda] called my wife [Terrin]—remember, our families were still in Tampa—at maybe like four in the morning, and said they couldn't get hold of Tim anymore, and the last time they talked to him he was incoherent and wasn't doing very well. Could I go check on him?" McKay said.

"So Terrin called me. I was not sick yet, and didn't know he was. I said, 'Come on, the guy broke his leg; he's taking pain pills. He probably is incoherent. Let him sleep.' I hung up the phone, and thought about it, and I didn't go check on him. I thought, 'Ah, he's all right.'

"About an hour later, I got sick. I thought I was going to die. Later, I packed my stuff up, and went down to the car to get ready for practice, and there's no sign of Ruskell. Now, I was nervous. So I called him on the cell, and oh, man, he was bad."

Ruskell misplaced or couldn't reach his crutches during the night, leading to further complications.

"Imagine breaking your leg, you're in a cast, you have to make it to the bathroom and you have to crawl to the bathroom because it was pitch dark and he didn't have his crutches," McKay said. "Then after he got sick, he felt better, and went back to bed. And it happened again. He said he didn't make it to the bathroom that time, and now the whole room is bad, just bad. It was bad. It was a bad day for Tim Ruskell."

It wasn't much better for McKay, and other front office officials.

Given Ruskell's predicament, they left him in the hotel with arrangements to have him picked up later as they went to practice. Isn't this a violation of some NFL brotherhood, leaving behind wounded soldiers?

"Tim had not met any of the scouts yet, and the first time he was going to meet any of them was at the Senior Bowl, where he broke his leg. So he was not happy," McKay said. "He was just not happy."

Upon entering the car, McKay noticed that Falcons chief administrative officer Ray Anderson looked like death-warmed-over. Vice president of player personnel Ron Hill was sick in another car. "The next thing I know, Bob McDonough [Blank's security attaché] came around the corner and said, 'Arthur's sick as a goat,'" McKay said. "I call Ruskell back, and said, 'Tim, are you sick?' He said, 'I've never been this sick.' So I realized it was food poisoning."

On to practice the Falcons battered brain trust went.

"I was in the end zone, kind of watching a few plays, and ESPN came up and they wanted to do a quick thing on Dan Marino being hired by the Dolphins. I said, 'No problem,'" McKay said. "So I put the [earpiece] on, and I'm [holding a microphone], and the guy's saying, 'We're going in five ... four ... three ...' and I said, 'Stop. I can't do this yet.' I gave them the things, and went, and left, and came back and we did it again.

"I put the thing on, and answered the question, and said, 'Dan will do a great job. He knows football ver...' and I just kind of stopped, and said, 'I gotta go.' Took the thing off, and told the camera man, 'And I'm not coming back.' I mean I was dying."

If the Falcons' newly formed front office was searching for signs of the future, all they found on their first trip together were bad omens—like a dance with the plague.

"We all kind of got together and got in the car and drove to the airport. I got sick on the interstate; we had to stop on I-10, going to the plane. It was bad," McKay said. "I'd had food poisoning before, but not like this, where I really thought this might be it; I might not make it. This may not happen. This may be over.

"We had a lot of things to do; we had a lot of things we had to get done. How many times can you, with a new boss, who you're trying to impress and be good around, a new coach, a new coordinator, say, 'Stop the car,' on the interstate. 'I've got to get out.' Terrin called me that night and said, 'You did what? You threw up on the interstate? That's not a good impression.'"

Everybody seemed to get over it—although Ruskell took a while longer.

"Tim was three cabins down from me at Lake Lanier [a complex near team headquarters where newly-hired Falcons officials stay until officially relocating]," McKay said. "I started playing *Driving Miss Daisy*. He'd come out in the morning on his crutches, I'd drive him into work."

James Daniels left Mobile that week wearing Pittsburgh gear, hired by the Steelers. Billy Davis departed in Giants gear; and one year later he was named defensive coordinator of the 49ers, filling Mora's old position. Harold Richardson left in street clothes.

Ruskell and McKay left a little of themselves in Mobile— ask them about it sometime.

The Seahawks made Ruskell their president in late February of 2005. McKay is considered a strong candidate to one day succeed Paul Tagliabue as commissioner of the NFL.

# CHAPTER SEVEN

# At Long Last

The Falcons lost and lost for a couple months in 1966, although coach Norb Hecker scrapped the spy excuse after the first loss to the Rams. Things got so bad in that inaugural season, though, that when the Falcons were 0-7, coming off consecutive losses of 44-7 and 56-3, they officially lost their feathers.

While practicing aerial maneuvers, the team mascot—a real falcon—went up, up, and away. It didn't come back—flew the coop, just like that.

"My bird just chickened out," fretted avian trainer Mike Cady. "I have nothing more to say until we find him, and I get a chance to talk to him and get his side of the story."

As word filtered out about this, tips started coming in. Eventually, Cady followed one, and made his way from the Falcons' offices in Atlanta-Fulton County Stadium (they often practiced in nearby Cheney or Lakewood stadiums, downtown facilities used for years by the Atlanta Public School system for high school games) to Decatur.

There, in an Atlanta suburb some 10 or 12 miles east of downtown, was a hungry bird, perched on top of a Kraft food plant.

"I swung the lure around and around and blew the whistle a couple of times, and he came right to me," Cady said. "I knew that if I didn't get him in a couple of days he would turn into a hunter, and I'd never get him back."

The bird didn't help that Sunday, or the next, as the Falcons lost back-to-back games at home 49-17 and 19-7, falling to 0-9.

Three straight road trips were in order.

## THE WHEEL ROLLS

Running back Ernie Wheelright suffered in training camp, trying in vain to keep his Cadillac from being repossessed. He had no interest in being further humbled in the same season when the Falcons traveled to New York for the 10th game.

New York coach Allie Sherman and Giants officials failed to protect Wheelright in the expansion draft months earlier, and the Falcons selected him. He was cranky on the subject of Giants.

"That was a special team for him because that was the team that cut him loose and put him in the expansion draft," said former Falcons linebacker Tommy Nobis. "I think he really liked being a New York Giant. Going back ... it was a big thing for Ernie."

It was a big thing for many Falcons, too. The Giants weren't good, either, owners of a paltry 1-7-1 record. Even if most of their greats were gone, the Giants' legendary name—and that the game would be played in Yankee Stadium—was a big deal to many of Atlanta's younger players.

"Well, back then, the exciting thing for a lot of us was that we were going to the big city. I had been to New York only one time up to that point. A lot of young men had never been there," Nobis said. "To get in that environment was exciting in itself.

"They couldn't grow any grass. The fields in multiuse stadiums back then weren't quite as bad as rodeo arenas, but they weren't nice. And the baseball stadiums, Wrigley [Field] in Chicago, Tiger in Detroit, Yankee Stadium, the fans were right on top of you.

"A cold day in November, smoke coming off the fans. They had blankets. When you think back on NFL football, it was one of those classic days. Back when we were growing up, on TV, if you saw TV, you saw the Yankees and Yogi Berra, Joe DiMaggio, Mickey Mantle. Or the Giants and [former quarterback] Y.A. Tittle. Suddenly, here I am in the same locker rooms! The locker rooms were old—really old. In the winter, in fact, if you weren't one of the first 10 or 15 guys in the shower, you weren't getting hot water in Yankee Stadium."

Wheelright wasn't concerned with that kind of stuff. Yes, he had a game to play, but he also had a show of sorts to attend, and he was going to be the star.

"He had rather long hair," Nobis said. "Friday after practice, he went to a stylist and he got his hair all done up. He had his best suit for the trip. You could tell he spent some money on his hair—it looked nice. I think he had dinner set up; we were allowed to go to dinner before our Saturday night meetings in those days.

"Anyway, Saturday morning he comes out to practice, and we're in sweats but we have to bring our helmets. He didn't have his helmet; he didn't want to mess up his hair. Coach Hecker called everybody over, and kind of put the heat on Ernie. He said, 'All right, we're going to let you practice without the helmet, but you have to have a heck of a game tomorrow.'"

Sherman had juggled his lineup that week, moving flanker Joe Morrison (the eventual head coach at the University of South Carolina) to running back, where he played well, rushing

17 times for 91 yards. "I just took it and ran like hell," he said afterward.

But the Falcons were better, and Wheelright had plenty to say about the outcome, rushing 14 times for 51 yards and catching five passes for 35 yards and two touchdowns. The Falcons beat the Giants 27-16 for the first win in franchise history. "Wheel stopped caring about his hair, put his helmet on and played hard," Nobis said.

Hecker said, "This was a game [Wheelwright] wanted badly."

The headline the next day in the now-defunct New York *World Journal Tribune* said, "Atlanta Takes Sherman as Wheel Turns It On."

"I was embarrassed by [being placed on the expansion list]," Wheelright said after the game. "Besides wanting to win, I wanted to show up Sherman. Why? Because I don't want anybody to ride me. I have a lot of pride. I'm a professional, and I know the better I do, the better I'll be paid."

Sherman got rode. The fans in Yankee Stadium were on him late in the game.

Atlanta *Daily World* sports editor Marion Jackson wrote:

*As the Falcons repulsed the final Giant threat, a deafening chant permeated the stadium and thousands of handkerchief-waving, disappointed and chagrined fans took up a chant: "Goodbye Allie, goodbye Allie, we're sorry to see you die." This mournful dirge and requiem for Allie was perhaps undeserved, but thus is the fortunes of war. One moment a hero, the next a goat, unwanted and unsung in an arena where once the crowds cheered. [sic]*

"I'll never forget that," Nobis said. "Here we are, playing the big New York Giants, with such tradition, and here we were the Atlanta Falcons, in our inaugural season, and they turned on their coach."

Rookie quarterback Randy Johnson, who'd lost his starting job earlier in the season only to regain it from Dennis Claridge, completed 15 of 27 passes for 177 yards and three touchdowns, running for another score.

It was more than the Falcons' first ever win; it was the beginning of a winning tradition. Atlanta is 7-1 all time against the Giants in New York, New Haven, and New Jersey—winning in Yankee Stadium (1966), the Yale Bowl (1974), and Giants Stadium (1982, 1998, 2002, 2003, 2004).

Hours after an estimated 1,200 fans greeted the Falcons at the airport as they returned to Atlanta, Hecker told the *Constitution*: "Yes, we came back down off Cloud Nine today. We looked at films, and at 11 o'clock this morning we quit thinking about the Giants. It's Bear week," he re-emphasized, meaning Papa Bear George Halas and all the big, bad Bears in the Chicago family.

"The Bears are a big, rough team with a lot of experience, a lot of age, a lot of savvy. This sounds ridiculous, but teams have been laying for us. Nobody wanted to be the first to lose to us. Our victory relieves the pressure on us. The Bears and Steelers and others we play won't have the same psychology going for them."

## ONE DOWN, ONE UP

Before that game against the Bears, the Chicago *Daily News* examined the Falcons' roster, which was replete with Midwesterners, and analyzed like this:

*Look behind the faceguards in those Confederate uniforms in Wrigley Field Sunday, and you'll find a troop of darn Yankee turncoats.*

The Falcons lost 23-6 at Chicago.

A week later, the Falcons beat the Vikings 20-13 in the snow. In that game, rookie safety Bob Riggle recovered a fumble on Minnesota's 1-yard line. He also intercepted two passes on a day when future Falcon quarterback Bob Berry threw five as Minnesota coach Norm Van Brocklin showcased his third-string quarterback for a possible off-season trade, or so he said.

Riggle, who returned one interception for a touchdown, was the last player selected in the rookie draft—going in the

20th round. "Bob Riggle didn't get much of a bonus when we signed him, but he'll get it when he signs again for next season," owner Rankin Smith said after the Vikings game. "You can put that in print."

## MUST'VE BEEN THE SHOE

You can argue the Falcons' biggest win in 1966 came when they upset the Cardinals 16-10 on December 11 for their first regular-season victory in Atlanta-Fulton County Stadium. St. Louis, which owned the league's top-ranked defense, was in position to tie Dallas for first in their division.

The keys were Atlanta's stiff defense and offensive guard-turned-kicker Lou Kirouac, who'd been through a tough stretch leading up to the game. Against St. Louis, though, he made field goals of 26, 47, and 14 yards (at the time when goal posts were on the goal line, not on the back line 10 yards deeper).

Then, reminiscent of Mars Blackmon, Kirouac deflected the praise away from his kicking leg.

"Must have been the shoe," Kirouac said afterward. "I changed for this game, going back to a smaller one I'd used before."

Atlanta's third victory tied the Vikings' record, set in 1961, for most wins in a team's first season, and Nobis played well while squaring off against Cardinals running back Johnny Roland. They ended up splitting all the major Rookie of the Year awards.

"As far as I'm concerned, there was nothing personal involved," Nobis said. "I've known Johnny ever since high school. He was at Corpus Christi, and I was in school in San Antonio, so we're old friends."

# LOCAL FLAVOR

It was "Tech and Georgia Day" for the Falcons' season finale. Former University of Georgia quarterback Preston Ridlehuber—who'd been on Atlanta's taxi squad all season—was signed for the game and caught the first pass thrown to him for a touchdown, later adding three more catches and one touchdown as a running back. He rushed four times for 23 yards.

Former Georgia Tech standout Taz Anderson, the tight end who'd battled knee problems early in the season, caught two touchdowns as well, as Atlanta scored a season-high 33 points.

The problem was, the defense never caught on to what the Steelers were doing, and Pittsburgh blasted Atlanta 57-33.

"That young man [Ridlehuber] has been hard to coach, but he's a comer," Falcons assistant Tom Fears said after the game. "He's wanted to play every week, and every week he's come to me pleading for the chance. I said, 'Riddlehouser—that's what I call him—just wait, the sun will shine. He's gonna be all right, that one. A lot of determination, good speed, and a desire that could put him in orbit."

Orbit, schmorbit. That sun never shone again.

Ridlehuber's Falcons career lasted for that one game—he was cut the following summer.

In the off season after the 1966 season, owner Rankin Smith hired his longtime financial assistant, Frank Wall, as the Falcons' general manager, even though his only football experience had been time served as the Falcons' treasurer.

This was the closest thing to a pivotal point in the first prolonged dark period in Falcons history.

Wall helped pull the trigger on the first trade in team history, according to the team's 2004 media guide, sending the Falcons' first-round pick, number three overall, to San Francisco in exchange for veterans Bernie Casey, Jim Wilson, and Jim Norton.

Casey, a wide receiver, never reported to the team. Wilson, an offensive lineman from the University of Georgia—spent most of his only season with the Falcons on the taxi squad. Norton, a defensive lineman, barely played in two Atlanta seasons.

The 49ers used the pick to select Heisman Trophy-winning quarterback Steve Spurrier of the University of Florida. One pick later, Miami chose Purdue quarterback Bob Griese, who went on to the Hall of Fame.

None of the 16 players chosen in the 1967 draft ever played a down for Atlanta. Not one.

Hecker's team came within a point of a winless second season. A 21-20 victory over the Vikings and rookie head coach Bud Grant, in Atlanta, was all that stood between a 0-13-1 record and abject infamy. The Falcons were outscored 422-175.

Three fans were arrested for running on the field the day of the 1967 finale. At least one, Decatur's Maxie Price—then 31— went big-time. He became a prominent car dealer in metro Atlanta.

Hecker made it three games—all losses—into the 1968 season before he was fired with a career record of 4-26-1. In the 18 games before his firing, Atlanta was 1-16-1.

His replacement? Van Brocklin, who'd driven the Vikings to a combined mark of 29-51-4 from 1961-1966.

# CHAPTER EIGHT

# Off and Running

Just four weeks after his scintillating 2002 debut as the Falcons' full-time starting quarterback, Michael Vick was on the bench. A strained right (non-throwing) shoulder suffered in a 20-6 loss to Tampa Bay kept him out of Atlanta's road game against the Giants.

Doug Johnson came to the rescue, though, and the Falcons won in Giants Stadium, 17-10, to postpone their obituary. A loss would've left Atlanta 1-4—the win gave the Falcons hope and set the stage for Vick.

So he did what we expect of stars—he dominated.

The Falcons didn't lose for two months—posting a 7-0-1 record over that span. In the process, Vick proved himself as the NFL's most exciting player. He did things no pro quarterback is supposed to do: he ran like a running back while effortlessly tossing laser-like passes to help everybody remember that he plays quarterback.

In his first game back, the Falcons ripped the Panthers—30-0—and Vick led the way by completing 16 of 22 passes for 178 yards and a touchdown. He also rushed for 91 yards, including a 44-yard dash down the right sideline that left both fans and defenders breathless.

His speed—reportedly in the low 4.3-second range over 40 yards—was staggering enough. The fact he seemed able to reach top speed so quickly was even more amazing. Suddenly, the Falcons were back at .500, and others were lining up in awe.

"There's not many quarterbacks in the league that can outrun an entire defense," said Carolina rookie linebacker Will Witherspoon. "He's pretty close to a cheetah."

Cheetahs, however, rarely slide. Vick was so on point in that game, however, that he even slid to avoid a tackle at one point. That was big news at the time because the 22-year-old previously refused to slide for fear of hurting himself. Turns out he wasn't very good at it, let alone comfortable trying it. On that day, though, it was obvious that his time spent a week earlier with Braves coach Terry Pendleton—who, as a member of the 1991 Atlanta Braves National League championship squad, was the league's Most Valuable Player—had paid off.

Vick played the role of student well, although he still doesn't slide very often. "I learned a lot, but I was sliding on my left side, you know, with my left leg starting off," he said. "[Sunday] I slid on my right side, so I like that a little better. I wasn't scared. I just did it."

Nike loved that. Vick's contract with the shoe giant would only get bigger. But that would come later. For now, he was just getting started.

A week later, at New Orleans, the Falcons trailed the Saints 35-34 as they took over with 2:12 left in the game. The ball was on Atlanta's 11-yard-line, and the Falcons had no timeouts left when Vick got busy.

*Michael Vick ran like a running back, a very fast one, and threw bullets effortlessly upon becoming a full-time starter in 2002. His 777 rushing yeards were third most in NFL history for a quarterback.*

"He just came in the huddle and said, 'Let's win. Let's win,'" former wide receiver Shawn Jefferson said. "It was like he'd been here before, and seen the way it was going to go."

Vick, who earlier threw a ball into the upper deck of the stands after scoring a touchdown, completed four of six passes (the incompletes were spikes to stop the clock) for 48 yards, and rushed twice for 14 yards.

Having run himself sick, he benched himself for the final two plays. "I thought I was going to vomit," Vick said. "I didn't want to throw up on the field."

Moments later, Jay Feely made a game-winning kick.

"You hear people talking about MVP," Jefferson said. "Nobody in this league means more to their team than Michael. When the chips are down, and you're staring defeat in the face, that's when quarterbacks are measured."

Longtime left tackle Bob Whitfield couldn't help but be impressed. "That dude carried Chapstick in his helmet. That's the coolest cat on the planet," Whitfield said. "He's the only guy I know who will curse you out in a soft voice."

As No. 7 solidified his legend in Atlanta, the NFL noticed. A few days after the stirring 37-35 win in the Superdome, the league fined Vick $5,000 for wearing his socks incorrectly, and $2,500 for throwing the ball in the stands. A couple days after that, the league retracted the fines, and warned Vick not to make either mistake again.

## HIGH-WIRE ACT

Up to 5-3 after a narrow win over Baltimore in which the Ravens bounced Vick around like a pinball, the Falcons' new division rivals were taking note as well (the NFL realigned divisions in 2002).

In Tampa Bay, the Bucs were on their way to winning their first Super Bowl. But long before anybody knew they'd emerge from the NFC South to win it all, the Bucs' former general manager could hardly contain his amazement over what Vick was doing.

On November 10, Rich McKay watched Atlanta's game at Pittsburgh on television. The Falcons were being smoked—34-17—with 12:32 left in regulation. Then Vick did it again. Overall, he completed 24 of 46 passes for 294 yards, and one passing touchdown. He also carried 10 times for 52 yards, scoring on an 11-yard run with 42 seconds left in regulation to force overtime. That play came on third-and-10, and Vick somehow escaped around the left end.

By then, he had thrown for first downs on third-and-22, third-and-23, and third-and-24 on a day when the rest of the NFL—or at least anybody who didn't realize it already—saw something special brewing in Atlanta.

"You may make one or two of those in a year," coach Dan Reeves said. "We make three in one game. Mike gives you the ability to do that by scrambling around. It motivates everybody. It motivates your defense, who may be playing awful, but [they think], 'If we just get the ball back, Mike's going to give us a chance to win.'"

McKay was astonished. "I remember watching the game, and it was over. Pittsburgh was going to win by like 17 points, and all of the sudden the comeback started, and he made some incredible runs and some incredible throws, made every play he needed to make to get the game to overtime. That was one of those games where you said, 'Uh-oh; the game is never over.' He can change it instantly. That's a rare ability. You can take most quarterbacks, you can play by the rules, play soft [in the secondary], and he has to check it down. Michael, with his strong arm, and the feet he has, those rules don't necessarily apply."

McKay, who has scouted thousands of college and pro players, could remember seeing just one player who presented such a game-breaking threat on each play.

"In Tampa, we faced it every year in Barry Sanders. I thought the skill he brought to the position was so different," McKay said. "Every time you played him you just thought, 'Oh, God, just let us survive the game.' He could change a game in the blink of an eye. You could defend, defend, defend, and then—game over. Barry was so hard to play against, as is

Michael, because you think you've got the game in hand, and he goes 60 yards and just changes everything."

## IN THE PANTHERS' HEADS

A 24-17 win over the Saints pushed Atlanta to 6-3-1 and sent the Falcons to Carolina. It was over once it started. For the second time that season, Atlanta blanked the Panthers, winning 41-0 as Vick completed 19 of 24 passes for 272 yards and two touchdowns. He didn't even have to run that day, and afterward Dr. Z (Paul Zimmerman) of *Sports Illustrated* suddenly had the Falcons atop his weekly NFL rankings with a record of 7-3-1.

Yet the most memorable run of Vick's young career came the next week.

In overtime, he took off around left end on an aborted pass attempt, and went 46 yards for the game winner at Minnesota. Vick set an NFL rushing record for quarterbacks that day with 173 yards, scoring twice, as Atlanta moved to 8-3-1 with their eighth straight game without a loss.

Vikings defenders had underestimated Vick's speed. In overtime, as two Minnesota players seemed to draw a bead on the young quarterback, Vick kicked into a higher gear. The defenders collided at Vick's backside and lay on the field as he scurried into the end zone, tossed the ball in celebration, and sprinted directly into the locker-room tunnel.

"Coming out of the pocket, when I saw the [defenders] downfield, they had their backs turned, and ... I knew I had the opportunity to run it," Vick said. "One of my greatest attributes is my vision. What I see looking downfield, I see so clearly. I take an angle I know guys can't get me at. That's what I was trying to do out there. I'm just thinking end zone all the way."

Others were thinking, "Vick was amazing."

"I watch all the Falcons games just because of him," Steve Sabol, president of NFL Films, told *The Atlanta Journal-Constitution*. "He's one of the guys who ... extends the parameters. Watching him is like watching a flashlight burning in a dark room; he's all you see. Somebody once wrote that about Willie Mays. That's what I was thinking [Sunday]."

Former Falcons cornerback Deion Sanders, who happens to know something about speed, was an analyst for CBS at the time.

"It seems like the game slows down when he's running, but it's not," Sanders said. "They're all playing at full speed. He's just that much faster, and he has vision—that's what people don't understand—while he's running the ball. It's unbelievable, and it goes unmentioned."

Another Atlanta legend, former Hawks star Dominique Wilkins, had this to say: "Guys like that, I pay to watch. It seems very easy for him. It was the same thing with [Michael] Jordan when he came in. Jordan made it seem easy the way he did it."

Offensive line coach Pete Mangurian may have said it best. "He's the X factor. It's like he's playing in the back yard with his little brothers."

## CASHING IN

After the Vikings game, Vick's name arose in many MVP award discussions.

Former Chiefs and Bills head coach Marv Levy wrote this for NFL.com: "Every now and then, someone comes along in each sport who jumps above players who were thought to be among the elite. We saw Michael Jordan do that in basketball, and I saw Joe DiMaggio do that in baseball when I was younger. It's too early to say that Michael Vick is that kind of player, but with all the great players to have at quarterback, he has abilities that stand out even in comparison to the best. He might not be unstoppable, but he continues to prove how amazing he is."

But Vick had a stomach virus the week after the Minnesota game, and the Falcons lost three of their last four games in 2002, including a lopsided 34-10 blowout at Tampa Bay one week after the Minnesota game.

*Vick's 46-yard game-winning run in overtime at Minnesota came on a day when he rushed for 173 yards, an NFL single-game record for a quarterback.*

Luckily, Atlanta made the playoff cut before they finished their game at Cleveland in the season finale—a game where they failed to score in four attempts from the doorstep of the Browns' goal-line in the final moments. The Saints also lost that day to grant the Falcons a wildcard berth.

Vick, though, was winning at the cash register.

His jersey sales were No. 3 in the NFL by the end of that season, and his commercial opportunities were lining up. Shortly after being drafted first overall in 2001, he signed long-term deals with Coca-Cola (working chiefly with the company's PowerAde sports drink) and Nike. Nabisco was suddenly interested in his services, and EA Sports came calling for a deal that would eventually land him on the 2003 cover of the company's wildly popular *Madden* football game series.

# HELL FREEZES, LAMBEAU THAWS

Most Falcons fans might've worried that their trip to the postseason would be a one-and-out scenario given that their team was just 7-9 in 2001 and had a quarterback in 2002 who was a first-time (albeit full-time) starter.

Besides that, Atlanta had to play a first-round game at Lambeau Field, where the Packers were 11-0 in postseason games. Plus, with quarterback Brett Favre at the helm, the Packers were 35-0 in games when game-time temperature was 35 degrees or colder.

It was below freezing that night in Green Bay, but Vick and his teammates had other ideas as they turned the team's first playoff game in nearly four years into one of the organization's top three moments of all time.

At 22, Vick played like you'd have expected Favre to play steadily. He made a few staggering plays, but didn't overwhelm Green Bay while completing a modest 13 of 25 passes for 117 yards and a touchdown to Jefferson on the game's opening possession. He rushed 10 times for 64 yards, making some magical moves in the falling snow as Atlanta raced to a 24-0 halftime lead.

Vick, who'd been sacked about once every 10 snaps during the regular season, wasn't sacked a single time.

At one point, Packers defensive end Khabeer Gbaja-Biamila chased Vick toward the Green Bay bench, in the backfield. Vick ducked under him as Gbaja-Biamila went for a sack. Then he turned upfield for an 11-yard gain on third-and-3. A Tampa Bay staff member who watched the game later said that Vick "almost had his helmet ripped off."

More to the point, Atlanta did not turn the ball over, and Green Bay, which had led the NFL with a plus-17 turnover margin in the regular season, coughed it up five times (two on Favre interceptions).

Vick's best friend on the team, former Virginia Tech teammate Keion Carpenter, had two interceptions from his free safety spot and tipped at least one more. "It's amazing what you can

*When the Falcons won at Green Bay, Michael Vick was super steady, and occasionally spectacular, as the Packers lost a playoff game at Lambeau Field for the first time in their history.*

accomplish when everybody tells you something can't be accomplished," he said. "The thing is that we never stopped believing in ourselves, even when everyone said we backed into the playoffs last week."

The Falcons' season ended the next week with a 20-6 loss at Philadelphia—Eagles cornerback Bobby Taylor returned one of Vick's two interceptions for a touchdown. Philadelphia benefited greatly when Vick's apparent touchdown run in the second half—a play that would've tied the scored at 13—was called back. Officials ruled that guard Travis Claridge—who was about 15 yards behind Vick—held a Philadelphia defender.

"I think they were nitpicking a lot of things," Claridge said.

Two plays later, Feely missed a 37-yard field goal.

Game over.

Season over.

# CHAPTER NINE

# The Dutch Oven

Van Brocklin is the kind of blunt soul who could, in a sudden burst of temper, make his mother feel that all the pains of childbearing are not worthwhile.

You've heard newspapermen grumbling about Hecker. He keeps them waiting outside. He spars with them, using clichés for a weapon. Or he turns on his heels and leaves them standing there with their tongues hanging out.

I'm not altogether certain that a man who has had his chance at Vince Lombardi and Paul Brown—admittedly their rates were high—and turned them both down, can be expected to receive Van Brocklin with the enthusiasm I do. Rankin Smith has only to deal with him holding the whip in hand. In my case, it's without sword or even a shield.

*I'm willing to take the chance. Bring him on, even if he does have a disposition like Hitler with a hangover.*

—Furman Bisher
*The Atlanta Journal*

There was no thought among the Falcons of making the playoffs in the midst of the 1968 season. For the players, the coaches, and even the fans, it was about survival.

Head coach Norb Hecker had a career record of 4-26-1 when owner Rankin Smith fired him three losses into the team's third season. Before Norm Van Brocklin—a Hall of Fame quarterback for the Los Angeles Rams and Philadelphia Eagles and former Vikings coach—was even hired, rumors of his impending arrival—and temper—preceded him.

Nobody could've imagined how prophetic *Journal* sports editor/columnist Furman Bisher was when he wrote the excerpt above about the man who would become the Falcons' second head coach.

Van Brocklin, also known as "The Dutchman" in honor of his heritage, had quite a reputation as a tactician. Given his nature as a hothead, he might have been known better as "The Dutch Oven."

When he was coach of the Vikings from 1961-1966, he battled with reporters, once coming to blows with Jim Klobuchar. The Minneapolis sportswriter later wrote: "Unless a reporter has five fights per season with the Dutchman, he isn't doing his job."

Fran Tarkenton knew the wrath of Van Brocklin. In fact, when the Falcons played in their first season at Minnesota, Van Brocklin—in his last season as Vikings coach—benched his star quarterback. Van Brocklin knew well that the game would be televised back in Georgia—Tarkenton grew up in Athens and played at the University of Georgia. He explained that backup Bob Lee needed some work as an excuse, but Atlanta beat Van Brocklin and the Vikings, 20-13.

After that season, Tarkenton wrote a letter to Minnesota management saying he would not play for Van Brocklin—virtually demanding to be traded. He was sent to the Giants, and Van Brocklin resigned—partly to protest the fact that team officials sided with the quarterback.

The Dutchman's first game back after a year-plus hiatus was a disaster as the Falcons fell to the Packers in their fourth game of the 1968 season 38-7. Coincidentally, Atlanta's 11-game losing streak ended at Tarkenton's expense as the Falcons defeated the visiting Giants 24-21 in Van Brocklin's second game with Atlanta.

In less than a month, the new coach cut six veterans, five of them at least part-time starters—including Jim Norton, the last player from the ill-fated 1967 trade with the 49ers. Van Brocklin took control over the roster in the face of local criticism. The Falcons' front office, led by former CPA Frank Wall, didn't seem to have a clue what it was doing.

One assistant coach quit within a week of Van Brocklin's hiring, and he fired five more the day following a 2-12 season.

Van Brocklin compared Atlanta's offensive line to marshmallows, and proceeded to draft Notre Dame tackle George Kunz with the No. 2 pick, passing on running back Leroy Keyes (Browns) and eventual Hall of Fame defensive tackle Joe Greene (Steelers).

The greatest highlight of his second season, in 1969, came in a 45-17 win over the Saints, when reserve running back Harmon Wages—formerly the backup to Heisman Trophy-winning quarterback Steve Spurrier at the University of Florida—ran for a 66-yard touchdown, passed 16 yards to Paul Flatley for a touchdown, and caught an 88-yard touchdown pass from Bob Berry.

The touchdown reception and touchdown run set franchise records. But even with a three-game winning streak at the end of the season, the Falcons finished 6-8 in 1969, and 1970 was worse. They finished 4-8-2.

## PUT UP YOUR DUKES

True to his legend, Van Brocklin was explosive to say the least. At training camp in the summer of 1971—while at Furman University in Greenville, South Carolina—he went at it with another reporter, Frank Hyland of *The Atlanta Journal.*

The coach actually invited disaster, suggesting that reporters join him and the coaching staff one evening after practice for dinner at Ye Olde Fireplace—a local establishment.

Apparently, there was some name-calling, and Hyland—a grizzled reporter if ever there was one—later reported that Van Brocklin called him a "whore writer."

Then, it went something like this:

*"When I write, I am a winner,"* Hyland responded. *"You are a loser."*

*"I am not,"* Van Brocklin said.

*"Check your record,"* the reporter said.

Van Brocklin didn't have any reference materials with him, so he unsurprisingly took offense to the comment. Reaching across a table, he grabbed Hyland by the necktie and started yanking. Bisher later wrote that Hyland began to turn purple. Hyland later wrote that Van Brocklin tore his jacket in three places and never bought him a new one.

The men quickly retreated to a hallway outside the dining area, but assistant coaches Billy Ray Barnes, Bob Griffin, and Fred Bruney intervened, perhaps saving Van Brocklin's job.

The next day, Van Brocklin said, "We got out and started smart-alecking around, and these things just happen. I'm the one who initiated the physical part of it, I'm sorry to say. As far as I'm concerned, it's all over now."

Oddly, this preceded the Falcons' first winning season. They went 7-6-1 in 1971.

# WINNING WAYS AND WHORE DAYS

A 7-7 record in 1972 kept the wolves at bay, so to speak, but not even the best season in Falcons history was remotely peaceful. The Falcons put together the first great streak in their existence in 1973, but Van Brocklin left craters along the way, and he was downright flammable at the beginning of the season.

After routing the Saints 62-7 to begin the season, Atlanta lost two straight games by a combined margin of 62-6.

Van Brocklin threatened to fine players $1,000 if they said anything negative to the media. With a 1-2 record, he locked reporters out of the locker room a few days before their upcoming game against the 49ers.

*The Atlanta Journal's* Ron Hudspeth wrote: "That [player fines] became a mere technicality Friday. The players would've needed leather lungs or a carrier pigeon to say anything negative or otherwise Friday."

No matter, the Falcons lost again, falling 14-9 to the 49ers.

Several hours after that game, *Constitution* columnist Jesse Outlar was mugged in the parking lot outside Atlanta-Fulton County Stadium. He was shot in the abdomen. "I felt no pain, but my legs were paralyzed. I couldn't move them," he said later. "Let me say this: it never occurred to me, standing there in broad daylight, that the guy would shoot."

Fans, meanwhile, were ready to shoot their team. Another strange thing happened the next Sunday, and it wasn't the banner in Atlanta Fulton County Stadium the next week that read: *"My Wife, My Money, Even My Ole Hound ... I'll Trade Them For Just One Falcon Touchdown."*

The Falcons whacked the Bears 46-6, as former Minnesota quarterback Bob Lee—who'd replaced the injured Dick Shiner a week earlier against the 49ers—completed 11 of 13 passes for 181 yards and two touchdowns, and backup Pat Sullivan, the former Auburn star, completed six of seven for another 76 yards.

Soon Shiner was cut. As the Falcons won three straight games, the city was abuzz, and the head coach was frequently fuming—and saying strange things.

Alex Hawkins, a member of the original Falcons team, had a regular column in the *Journal*. After a 17-3 win over the 49ers moved Atlanta's record to 4-3, Van Brocklin commented on Hawkins's peculiar breed of journalist.

"Every city has one, a former player who prostitutes himself by writing for a newspaper," he said. "Now we have one, too. A whore writer."

As strange as it might seem, hardly anybody was surprised by this. Van Brocklin wasn't afraid to say anything. A staunch Republican who adored president Richard M. Nixon and seemed convinced that everything wrong in the world was the fault of Communists; he frequently ridiculed players whom he considered liberal.

Despite a general disdain for the media, he would openly share his political views at times: "Can you imagine [George] McGovern or [Ted] Kennedy as president? We might as well ship the White House over to Red Square."

A week later, rookie kicker Nick Mike-Mayer hit five field goals in a 15-13 upset of the division-leading Rams—whom Van Brocklin quarterbacked to glory in the 1950s. He followed that with a win over another former employer as the Falcons won in Philadelphia, 44-27.

Talk of the team's first playoff berth filled the air as Fran Tarkenton—who'd been traded back to the Vikings—and Minnesota arrived in Atlanta for a Monday night game on November 19, 1973.

With Braves slugger Hank Aaron—sitting one home run shy of Babe Ruth's career record of 714—joining announcers Howard Cosell, Don Meredith, and Frank Gifford in the broadcast booth, Atlanta took advantage of Tarkenton's injury as they won 20-14.

A 28-20 win over the Jets and quarterback Joe Namath, the Falcons' seventh straight victory, left Atlanta 8-3, and giddy ... until the bottom fell out.

The Falcons needed to win two of their final three games—all of which were at home—to make the playoffs. Two of those games would be against lousy teams: St. Louis and New Orleans.

First, though, Bills running back O.J. Simpson gashed the Falcons for 137 rushing yards on his way to an NFL single-season record of 2,003 yards. Buffalo rushed for 289 yards overall in a 17-6 win.

Still the Falcons were in decent shape, especially with the 3-8-1 Cardinals coming to town without injured quarterback Jim Hart and with one of the league's worst pass defenses.

However, Lee completed just three of 16 passes for 26 yards, and eventually Sullivan replaced him. St. Louis rookie quarterback Gary Keithley was better than he had a right to be, and Cardinals kicker Jim Bakken kicked six field goals on the way to a 32-10 win that sank the Falcons.

"We couldn't scratch our butts," Van Brocklin said. That was mild compared to the coach's suggestion that someone else was scratching the Falcons' butts.

Asked about the Falcons' problems, the coach said, "What's the matter with them? All the Peachtree whores and bartenders have been telling them how good they are."

That would haunt Van Brocklin, whose team won a meaningless season finale over the Saints 14-10 to finish 9-5. If the Redskins had lost that day, and they were trailing the Eagles 10-0 at one point, Atlanta still would've made the postseason. But Washington rallied to wail on the Eagles 38-20.

To add insult to injury, Dave Hampton finished just shy of 1,000 rushing yards for the second straight season. In 1972, he hit 1,000 on the nose against the Chiefs, but lost six yards on the next play—although he gained one more, he was stuck at 995. In '73, he need just 15 yards to become the Falcons' first ever 1,000-yard rusher. He got 12, finishing at 997.

"At least we were two yards better this year," said center Jeff Van Note.

## SETTING A TABLE FOR DISASTER

Although he was notoriously combustible, Van Brocklin's strong 1973 season appeared to leave him in solid shape. Then again, as with Nixon—who was embroiled in the early stages of the Watergate conspiracy—his wheels were about to come off.

Up to that point, since no players had publicly challenged Van Brocklin, he stood on stable ground in the eyes of owner Rankin Smith. Yet the coach was just as harsh and hard to deal with in a closed-door meeting as he was with players.

In the off season, late in February of 1974, guard Andy Maurer told his hometown newspaper, the Medford (Oregon) *Mail-Tribune*: "I think the Falcons have everything you need to win a championship. It's just a matter of the players getting old enough where they will ignore Van Brocklin."

This comment and others were picked up by the newspapers back in Atlanta. Once many of them were printed in the *Journal* and the *Constitution*, the seeds for Van Brocklin's exit were officially sown.

"At Atlanta, we have one idea—Van Brocklin's," Maurer said. "He considers every player except Tommy Nobis to be a ?#&*. Norman operates by the double standard. He says what he wants to say, and if the players say what they want to say, they get fined $1,000. The Peachtree whores didn't beat us; St. Louis did. My question is, if we can't pop off, why should Norm be allowed to? Sure, I'd like to be traded. I'm tired of playing for Van Brocklin."

Soon there were reports that running back Art Malone, among others, desired a trade. Smith decided to have president Frank Wall negotiate player contracts—taking over a task Van Brocklin had been handling. This improved nothing.

During a player strike in the summer of 1974, Van Brocklin—himself a former player rep while with the Eagles— was critical of players who picketed.

Players were seeking several things, including free agency, the right to veto trades, and that disciplinary powers of coaches and owners be diluted. Nobis was among the players to hold out originally, although he made it clear in public statements that he didn't think it was the right thing to do, and that he was doing so to support teammates who were in the majority.

Eventually, before the strike ended, several players, including Nobis, eventually broke the picket line. "At times, I wanted to side with my coach, and at times I wanted to side with my teammates," he said 31 years later. "Dutchman had a tough time with that because the players wanted to know why."

The end of the strike did not soothe raw nerves; it brought instead another round of angst.

Before the season began, Maurer and defensive back Ken Reaves, the Falcons' player representative, were traded to New Orleans. Once the season started, and the Saints beat Atlanta 14-13 to drop the Falcons to 0-3, Reaves—widely respected by his former teammates—said: "Maybe if the Falcons continue to lose, they'll lose one of the greatest spirit killers in the history of the game—Norm Van Brocklin."

Although their head coach relaxed some of his rules in 1974—allowing facial hair for the first time for example—he was still a bear.

Less than a month later, the Saints beat the Falcons again, 13-3, and the coach blamed the strike for his team's 2-4 record. "That's when it all started. That %*@#ing strike, those radical @#$%s," Van Brocklin said. "It's affected the whole league. I haven't seen a good football team this year."

Next, Malone and Al Dodd—and perhaps others never reported—quit the team, and Wall had to talk them into returning.

Soon, the despondent Falcons were 2-5. A day after their fifth loss, The Dutchman told reporters, "I'm a #$%@ing fighter. I'm not going to lie down for anybody. Frankly, this morning I feel embarrassment. I've got pride and loyalty and it hurts me."

At roughly the same time, the U.S. Supreme Court ruled the Falcons had to refund about $400,000 for advance ticket sales in 1971 because the government said their 1971 ticket price hike was in violation of wage and price controls.

Asked what a coach could do to improve his team's plight, Van Brocklin suggested, "Go have a beer."

## LOSING GROUND FAST

As he raged, some of Van Brocklin's friends had little choice but to watch in horror. Former USC coach John McKay, who was Van Brocklin's college roommate at Oregon, said, "If anything happened to me or my wife, I wouldn't trust my kids with anybody but Norm Van Brocklin. With him, I know they would be safe. His biggest fault has been his honesty."

Van Brocklin and his wife, Gloria, had four sons and adopted two daughters. Those who lived near his family's farm in Social Circle—east of Atlanta—said he was a good, but private neighbor.

Yet, as Bob Dylan sang, the times were a-changing, and the coach had a hard time keeping up.

"Van Brocklin was tough … very brilliant, very smart, caught up in the evolution of our game," Nobis said in 2005. "You look at the Vietnam time, and there was rebellion against a lot of things. Even in the NFL, young players started to ask a lot of questions of the coaches … why are we having to run 10 wind sprints?

"At that point in our lives, people were asking more questions. Young men who were starting to challenge authority. Before that, say the 'old man,' and you could be referring to your dad, the teacher, your coach … but if the 'old man' told you to do it a certain way, you did, or you tried. It was that way at school, at home, and at work. When the 'old man' speaks now, a lot of times he gets challenged.

"Early on in my life, the way I was brought up, if you challenged the 'old man,' there was a belt or a paddle or whatever. You didn't challenge very often. The Dutchman was caught right at a time in the NFL where times were changing, and coaches needed better answers and needed to tolerate a little more."

## STACKING FURNITURE FOR GOOD

A 42-7 road loss to the defending Super Bowl champion Dolphins on November 3 dropped the Falcons to 2-6. The Dutchman's tolerance had reached its end.

After that loss, Van Brocklin concluded a very brief press conference by saying, "That's it, boys. Don't let the door hit your asses on the way out."

Folks weren't willing to put up with the head coach any more either. Owner Rankin Smith responded to questions about replacing Van Brocklin by saying he couldn't think of anybody else to hire.

In the radio booth after the Dolphins game, color man Billy Lothridge—the team's first punter—offered to take over on WQXI's airwaves. "I mean it, Jack [Hurst]," Lothridge said. "And if he can't find a coach … well, heck, I'll step out of my business for the rest of the year, and I'll coach the team myself."

At a news conference the next day, Hudspeth asked Van Brocklin if he was still a fighter.

"Try me out. Do you want to fight me? Hell yes, I'm a fighter," the coach said. "If any of you $*#%s want to fight, then let's stack furniture."

As he left the room, Van Brocklin said, "That's an open invitation."

One writer replied, "That's not my style."

"Well, it's mine," Van Brocklin said.

Smith soon fired his coach, although the team's owner stayed underground for a couple days before calling the *Constitution* and commenting.

"It was bitter," he said of the process of firing Van Brocklin, and naming defensive coordinator Marion Campbell coach rather than hire former Packers quarterback Bart Starr, who'd expressed interest in the job. "Nobody is general manager right now. Let's see, I guess Frank Wall can do that job."

Campbell fared no better, losing five straight games before Atlanta beat the Packers 10-3 in the season finale to finish 3-11.

"The only think I can think of that is in the same league with our season is Watergate," Hampton said after the final game. "You'd like to think the Dutchman business is behind us, but if you want some explanations, you can't run around it. We blew the playoff chance last December [in 1973]. He said some goofy things.

"We had the strike, and he traded the player representative, Kenny Reaves, the guy who kept our secondary together and was one of the most respected guys on the team. He traded Andy Maurer and tore up our offensive line. We got some people hurt, and we ran into quarterback trouble and before you knew it was a nightmare. Maybe the squad never got its character back."

When the *Constitution* sent a writer to visit Van Brocklin on his farm weeks after the firing, he had little to say. His wife, however, all but confirmed Nobis's theory that her husband had a hard time fitting in with the new-age players.

"For a period of time I think it has been going downhill, a reflection of Watergate and other ills of our society," she said. "All people have to do is check the tapes of last year's games and this year's. Some are just going through the motions. And it all traces back to last summer's strike."

# CHAPTER TEN

# Of Miracles, Mazzetti, and the Lord

Things didn't improve after Norm Van Brocklin was canned. Marion Campbell—Van Brocklin's defensive coordinator—took over and went 1-5 to finish out the 1974 season.

The Falcons traded offensive tackle George Kunz and their first-round draft pick to the Colts for the No. 1 overall pick of the 1975 draft, which they used to select Oregon State quarterback Steve Bartkowski. The fair-haired, strong-arm Bart-man would see many dark days, however, before light finally shined on his Falcons.

Soon after owner Rankin Smith was fired from his position as chief of the Life of Georgia insurance company, he gave Campbell the boot after a 1-4 start in 1976. Smith unwittingly chose general manager Pat Peppler as his new head coach—a man who repeatedly reminded people that he never wanted the job.

Peppler did no better. The Falcons lost six of nine games to finish the 1976 season, including a 59-0 loss at Los Angeles in the 13th game of the season as the Rams rushed for an NFL-record eight touchdowns. The axe fell on Peppler soon thereafter.

The Rams gave the Falcons their next coach. Assistant Leeman Bennett got the job after Georgia native Dan Reeves—the Cowboys' offensive coordinator—didn't get the nod. Years later, Reeves said he didn't want the job—suggesting that he was still too young at that time to be an NFL head coach. The dirt floor in the weight room under Atlanta-Fulton County Stadium and a contract offer outlined on a cocktail napkin didn't impress him either. In the 1998 Super Bowl season, Reeves assured reporters that he had no ill will years earlier when Bennett was chosen—although that might have been his stab at revisionist history.

This much was certain: Smith flew in Miami personnel director Bobby Beathard as a potential general manager after the 1976 season and asked him to interview two men as potential head coaches: Reeves and Bennett. Beathard did, and said that if he were hired as general manager, he would hire Reeves as his coach.

Smith turned around and hired Eddie LeBaron to be general manager, and LeBaron hired Bennett.

The Falcons went 7-7 in 1977, setting an NFL record by allowing just 9.2 points per game as the "Gritz Blitz" defense took shape with defensive ends Claude Humphrey and Jeff Merrow, linebacker Greg Brezina, and cornerback Rolland Lawrence. If not for another injury-plagued season for Bartkowski, the Falcons may have made the playoffs. This happened even though Nobis—the best defender in team history—retired after the 1976 season with bum knees. In 1978, they did make the playoffs for the first time, and it was a wild ride.

*Falcons founder Rankin Smith Sr. comfortably observes new hire, Leeman Bennett, who he signed as head coach before the 1977 season.*

# BATTLING BART

The first 39 seasons of Falcons football yielded little magic, although there were notable exceptions: the 1980 NFC West title, the 1998 Super Bowl appearance, and Jim Mora's first-year campaign resulting in a trip to the 2004 NFC Championship game.

And although the 1978 season surely qualified as the first hint of magic in team history, it was not due to Bartkowski's numbers. He completed just 50.7 percent of his passes, good for 10 touchdowns but 18 interceptions.

The Falcons also were outrushed 2,067 yards to 1,660, and outscored 290-240. That team had a habit of losing big, and winning close. Fortunately, they won nine times, and lost seven on the way to winning a wildcard spot in the playoffs.

Atlanta got there with a pretty good defense, an amazing rookie kicker named Tim Mazzetti—whom they plucked out of a bar during training camp—and quite the run of what some would call luck.

Hurdles popped up, though, and they involved big-timers.

Bartkowski's reputation as a playboy wasn't helped the summer before the season when he famously dated LPGA golfer Jan Stephenson. A picture of the pair even appeared in the Atlanta newspapers in June of that year.

"It's a lot easier to get interested in a woman who is considered a celebrity," he said at a tournament played near Cincinnati. "The only drawbacks are being recognized, and being thought of as a golf groupie."

As the team moved its headquarters from Atlanta-Fulton County Stadium about 30 miles northeast to the sleepy suburb of Suwanee, things got worse for Bart before they got better.

There was considerable debate in the media, and the public, when training camp began as to whether Bennett should start the oft-injured Bartkowski, a rookie of the year in '75 who'd come to be loathed by Atlanta fans—or June Jones III, who'd thrown one NFL pass ... for negative yardage.

In the preseason opener, Atlanta trailed 17-0 and Jones, competing with Kim McQuilken for the No. 2 job, rallied the Falcons to a 20-17 win over the Jets.

The Falcons' quarterback derby was front and center through the preseason. When Bartkowski was seen crying on the bench after a terrible performance, he was ridiculed far and wide.

A fan sent this poem to *The Atlanta Journal*, and it ran on August 25:

*They called him Golden Boy*
*He had gold locks of hair*
*And there was a day in Atlanta*
*When his name shone everywhere*
*He was the No. 1 quarterback*
*He was brought to the Falcons team*
*He would bring out of them, a dream*
*He could pass the ball like a rocket*
*His season was well on its way*
*He had all the potential of a star*
*He made Atlanta his home to stay*
*He led his team through victories*
*Till he lay hurt on the field in pain*
*Yet still with courage and faith*
*He cheered from the sidelines*
*On crutches in the rain*
*He never gave up on his team*
*He raised money for the crippled and the poor*
*He saw that people would smile again*
*Never once a fan he'd ignore*
*The season's exhibition games opened*
*Under a dark but dreary sky*
*Steve Bartkowski walked away*
*With a teardrop in his eye*
*His fans they booed his talent*
*The stands were full of animals crazed*

*Steve Bartkowski had his share of ups and downs in his first few years as the Falcons' quarterback.*

*They shouted for other quarterbacks*
*He stood there looking dazed*
*His voice cracked as press pushed toward him*
*Do you consider yourself No. 1?*
*His weakened soul and spirit*
*He was fighting now without a gun*
*He'd done the best he could*
*Through all the pain and sorrow he tried*
*That was the day Atlanta was cruel*
*Steve Bartkowski silently cried*

—Jackie Yaneva, Atlanta

Bartkowski turned inward, isolating himself as Bennett made Jones the starter.

"I have purposely avoided going anywhere," the former starting quarterback said. "I just don't want to hassle. It has affected the way I live. I find myself living in a shell. It's put handcuffs on me. I try not to look into people's faces when I go somewhere because then if they recognize me, I start acting differently. I can't be myself. It really got to me. I'm so fed up with everything. The situation last week was such a burden."

The Falcons won their regular-season opener 20-14, beating the Houston Oilers with the help of a blocked punt and two field goals.

## CLAUDE BAILS, BART'S BORN AGAIN

Before long, the Falcons were 1-3, and Bennett said: "You can write it, and people aren't going to believe it, but we're getting better every week."

After a 14-9 loss to the Bucs in which Claude Humprhey missed his man on a field goal attempt and Tampa Bay blocked the field goal and scored a touchdown for the winning margin, he quit. One of the league's premier pass rushers, and the Falcons' all-time sack leader with 94.5, Humphrey said he was retiring on September 27.

"I just couldn't do it anymore. I couldn't hate my opponents like I used to," said the six-time Pro Bowler, who became a radio announcer before returning to the game when the Falcons traded him to the Eagles a year later. "I couldn't get into the swing of things. I got up for the Houston game, but I couldn't get up for any of the others."

Humphrey's replacement—Jeff Yeates—played pretty well, as did the Falcons' new (old) quarterback.

Bartkowski was a new man, "reborn," he said, upon returning to the starting lineup for that loss to the Bucs.

"I've had a change of heart and mind since that first game. I guess you would say I was just pouting when I didn't start against Houston," he said. "I've changed my life since then. I had made the mistake of putting myself first. Now I'm putting the Lord first. I was at a low point in my life, and it seemed that everything was closing in on me. It's different now that I've reaffirmed my faith in the Lord. It has nothing to do with starting football games. You have to realize you shouldn't be number one, and Christ should be."

The Falcons split the next two games, overcoming a 14-0 deficit to the Giants to win 23-20 on the day the team honored Nobis, and losing 31-7 to the Steelers, who were on their way to a Super Bowl championship.

After the Giants game, Bennett said, "It was Bart's most outstanding game by far since I've been here. He made the plays a quarterback has to make for a club to be a winning one."

New York had the NFL's third-best offense, but managed just 135 yards against Atlanta. Bartkowski was steady.

"I just decided not to try and throw the ball into a crowd any more," he said. "I'd look as long as I could and then I'd tuck it in and go. I didn't run by design; I ran because I had to because I didn't want to throw the interceptions. Hey, I already have five. Today, I sacrificed going for the big play to stay away from the bad play."

*Claude Humphrey, the Falcons' all-time sack leader, quit the team early in the 1978 season. Two years later, he went to the Super Bowl with the Eagles.*

# ON A ROLL

As Bartkowski carved out a new niche for himself, the Falcons' kicker, Fred Steinfort, dug himself a hole he couldn't escape.

After the Steelers game—in which he missed two field goal tries—he was cut. He'd made just three of 10 field goals. Sitting in his black van in the parking lot after his release, he had an interesting exchange with a *Constitution* sports writer.

"No comment," he said four straight times, revving the engine after rolling down his window. "I'm no longer employed here. I have no obligation to you, and I have nothing to say."

Upon driving way, Steinfort bellowed, "My leg's fine."

Maybe so, but it was no match for that of his successor, Philadelphia bartender Tim Mazzetti. Actually, another Falcons kicker, Nick Mike-Mayer, had sent Mazzetti packing already. He was cut by the Eagles, beaten out by Mike-Mayer, who held nearly all Atlanta scoring and kicking records after playing for the team from 1973-77.

Anyway, after a tryout, Mazzetti—who'd grown up mostly in Brazil—was the man as the Falcons launched the first significant winning streak in franchise history, starting with a 14-0 win over Detroit. The defense was the difference that day as the Lions mustered just 22 rushing yards on 26 attempts, and leading rusher Dexter Bussey managed zero yards in 14 tries.

A week later, the pass defense and Mazzetti made the difference. San Francisco rushed for 206 yards, but quarterback Steve DeBerg was sacked five times by a bunch of mad blitzers. He completed just eight of 22 passes for 53 yards, and Mazzetti's 29-yard field goal with one second left was the difference in a 20-17 win.

"I've never been that nervous in my life, and I don't think I ever could be again," the new kicker said. "Except maybe if we make it to the Super Bowl.

After Bartkowski finished his third straight game without an interception, an anonymous teammate said: "He got Christianity or whatever, and that is a factor, but the main thing might be that he isn't playing a role anymore. He isn't out running the streets and chasing all the women on Peachtree. He might have discovered that isn't Steve Bartkowski at all, no matter what the buildup was when he first got here."

## MORE MAZZETTI

Bartkowski was injured in the next game, on a Monday night against the division-leading Rams. No matter—Mazzetti was ready.

He kicked five field goals in a 15-7 win. "What we did," Jeff Merrow later said, "was blitz the hell out of them."

The Falcons' fourth straight win—21-10 over the 49ers—left them 6-4, and made a believer out of *Macon Telegraph* columnist Harley Bowers.

"I have to admit that when Bennett was named head coach of the Falcons early last year I was disappointed," he wrote. "I had been pulling for Dan Reeves, an Americus native who was, and still is, a top assistant to Tom Landry in Dallas."

## "BIG BEN RIGHT"

The most famous play in Falcons' history was about luck—sort of.

After trailing the Saints 17-3, the Falcons pulled within 17-13 on November 12, but New Orleans was in the driver's seat late. The Saints recovered an onside kick and ran the ball three straight times. Then, surprisingly, New Orleans coach Dick Nolan tried another run rather than punt.

Yeates stopped running back Chuck Muncie cold on a sweep, dropping him for no gain.

Moments later, Bartkowski let fly with 19 seconds left in the game. The play was called, "Big Ben Right."

Wide receivers Wallace Francis and Alfred Jackson were in the right places. Francis batted the pass in the air, just shy of the goal line. Amid a cluster of players from both teams, Jackson

*On "Big Ben Right," Bertkowski explained, "You just throw it up and hope."*

caught it and waltzed in to complete a stunning 57-yard scoring play.

"I can still see that ball coming at me," said Saints safety Ralph McGill, no relation to the famous former editor in Atlanta.

"There was no primary receiver," Bennett said. "We just batted the ball around, and hoped someone would catch it. Seriously, that's what we do."

"You just throw it up and hope," Bartkowski said. "I was surprised. I was able to see the whole play, and my first reaction was, 'Praise the Lord.'"

The Saints weren't praising anybody a couple weeks later.

Atlanta's five-game winning streak ended with a 13-7 loss to the Bears, but two weeks after letting the air out of the Saints, they did the exact same thing again.

On third-and-one at the Saints' 25 with 16 seconds left, Atlanta trailed 17-13 once more. McGill jumped to intercept a Bartkowski pass, but side judge Grover Klemmer threw his penalty flag. He said rookie wide receiver Dennis Pearson, who'd changed his route to avoid contact, drew interference from New Orleans cornerback Maurice Spencer.

Even newspapers photos seemed to indicate there was no contact made with Pearson.

"I wasn't supposed to be there, and I didn't feel him hit me," Pearson said. "I was surprised when I saw the flag. If he hadn't thrown it, I wouldn't have complained."

"That official has to live with that call. I don't." Spencer said. "If it was interference, why didn't he throw the flag right then? But there was a definite hesitation. He who hesitates is lost, and that official is lost."

Soon, tight end Jim Mitchell scored on a one-yard touchdown pass from Bartkowski with five seconds left in the game. The Falcons won 20-17—the second time in three weeks that they beat the Saints by that score, and the third of four times that season they won by that exact score.

*Journal* columnist Furman Bisher wrote:

*"Need a miracle? Call the Falcons. Babies trapped in burning buildings? Flood waters rushing down upon your town? Your yacht in the path of an iceberg? Call the Atlanta Falcons."*

McGill was all but calling the Falcons names. Check out this muttering monologue he mumbled while sitting at his locker afterward:

"Twice in a row? Damn. To them? Damn. To the Atlanta Falcons. Damn. To Atlanta? Damn. Pass interference? Hey, there ain't no way the Atlanta Falcons are better than the New Orleans Saints. Not on paper. Not on the field. But this ... twice?"

## STAGGERING DOWN THE STRETCH

Through 2004, the Falcons had won just once in Cincinnati, in their first ever trip in 1971. The Queen City was no place for the Falcons to be in 1978, either, as they were crushed 37-7 in week 14 by the 1-12 Bengals. Bartkowski threw three interceptions—two were returned for touchdowns—including one by eventual Bears head coach Dick Jauron.

Fog grounded the Falcons' plane, leaving the team in town an extra night.

But six days later the Falcons socked one of the teams they were battling for a wildcard spot as Mazzetti swung his magic club once more.

His 32-yard field goal with no time on the clock gave the Birds yet another 20-17 win. Was it a miracle? You decide. Washington blocked Mazzetti's 37-yard try moments earlier as the game clock expired.

However, 18-year veteran Ron McDole was ruled to be off-sides—although Redskins coach Jack Pardee said his men moved when snapper Paul Ryczek moved the ball illegally.

After Mazzetti nailed the re-kick, cornerback Rolland Lawrence said: "I think we might be a little blessed, you know."

Even the kicker was amazed.

"I couldn't believe it," Mazzetti later said. "I didn't want to believe it. I was already getting ready to be depressed. I know

I'm going to have a few drinks myself. I've got to get my feet warm."

One headline back in Atlanta simply read: "Miracle IV."

In 1973, when the Falcons first had a shot at making the playoffs, they won their last game, but didn't get the help they needed from other teams, as Washington overcame an early Philadelphia lead to win and sew up a playoff spot.

It was the other way around in 1978. The Falcons got pasted 42-12 by the Cardinals and quarterback Jim Hart, who ran for two touchdowns and passed for three more. Atlanta got in, though, because the Bears beat the Redskins. Atlanta locked up a wildcard berth with a 9-7 record.

## THE POLE BOWL

With Bartkowski and Eagles quarterback Ron Jaworski set to meet in the Falcons' first playoff game, the media referred to the game as, "The Pole Bowl," in reference the quarterbacks' shared heritage. A cold, wet day made it feel like the game was played at the North Pole.

After trailing 13-0 on Christmas Eve, the Falcons rallied with two touchdown passes by Bartkowski in the final five minutes. His two scoring targets were his old standbys, Francis and Mitchell. They helped the Falcons overcome five Atlanta turnovers—including three fumbles—on a day when the Eagles coughed it up just twice, but rushed for a mere 53 yards.

However, like so many Atlanta games that season, this one came down to a kicker—albeit from the other team.

Mike-Mayer was injured a couple weeks earlier, and punter Mike Michel missed one of his two extra points. Then, with 13 seconds left in the game, he sent a 34-yard field goal try wide right—securing the victory for the Falcons.

Through binoculars in the press box, Nobis watched the fan-induced bedlam unfold. "There goes the goal post," he said. "Wonder what the [upcoming] Peach Bowl is going to do now."

Brezina, who continued to live in Atlanta after his playing days ended, was among those mobbed. "Those fans hit me harder than the Eagles did," he said. "But they deserved to be on the field. They've waited 13 years for this."

CBS announcer Johnny Unitas said: "They've got something going for them that other teams don't have. And I don't know of anybody I'd rather have on my side than the Lord."

Nobody was on the Falcons' side the next week. They squandered a 20-13 halftime-lead at Dallas even though quarterback Roger Staubach was knocked out of the game. That 27-20 loss would not be the only time Danny White did a late number on the Falcons in a playoff game, although a shanked John James punt set up the Cowboys' 30-yard game-winning drive in the fourth quarter to make it easier on Dallas.

# CHAPTER ELEVEN

# Chi-Chi Chimes In

Although he was the No. 8 overall pick of the 1992 draft, there was little about Bob Whitfield—just 20 years old when he left Stanford after his junior season for the NFL—that suggested his staying power. Sure, the one-eyed offensive tackle could play; but setting the franchise-record at 123 straight starts? Well, nobody counted on that ... .

Sure, he was athletic, but he looked awkward ... and lazy—although much of his sluggish practice manner was contrived. In the spring of 2005, eight months after the Falcons cut him, Whitfield had finished a season with the Jaguars and was contemplating an offer from the Giants which he later signed. Looking back, he discovered a few topics worth mentioning.

Like the nickname "Chi-Chi."

"Lord Jamal gave it to me," he said, invoking former Falcons running back Jamal Anderson, who along with former

Atlanta defensive end Chuck Smith became one of Whitfield's best friends. "Lord J gave me that name because at the time he thought that his gangster-ism was comparable to *Scarface*—the movie. He was [actor] Al Pacino, and Scarface's right-hand man was Chi-Chi. So, I became Chi-Chi. The funny thing was he gave me that nickname because he's the boss. He said, 'I can't call you Don Corleone, because that'd mean I'm making you the boss.'"

Whitfield drew the ire of Falcons fans late in his Atlanta career because he had the tendency to attract yellow flags. Throughout his career, he was never an outright leader—he was not the vocal kind of guy you saw pumping up teammates in games. Anderson had that right. Once he became the elder of the offensive line, he tacitly took the reins.

Whitfield was rarely silent though and almost never violent—although there are exceptions to any rule. One game day, in fact, Big Bob had enough of quarterback Bobby Hebert—so he whacked him.

"He was already bitching at [offensive tackle Antone Davis], and Antone was just taking it," Whitfield recalled, with a chuckle. "Then, my dude makes a nice move, and hits Bobby. On the sideline, he says, 'Whit, you better block him … stop acting like a punk bitch.'

"I said, 'What?' And I hit him right in the chin. And here comes Antone, and he's already pissed. Antone hits him in the back of the head. That shit was so funny."

Actually, it wasn't very funny at the time.

In that game, Hebert—who'd replaced Jeff George at quarterback after George and coach June Jones had a shouting match on the sidelines during a game earlier that season—threw six interceptions in a 34-27 loss in the Georgia Dome to the St. Louis Rams. The loss was Atlanta's 12th in the 3-13 season of 1996.

"You get me and Bobby in a room, we'll both laugh about it," Whitfield said.

Actually, Whitfield loved playing with Hebert—and another well-traveled quarterback, Billy Joe Tolliver.

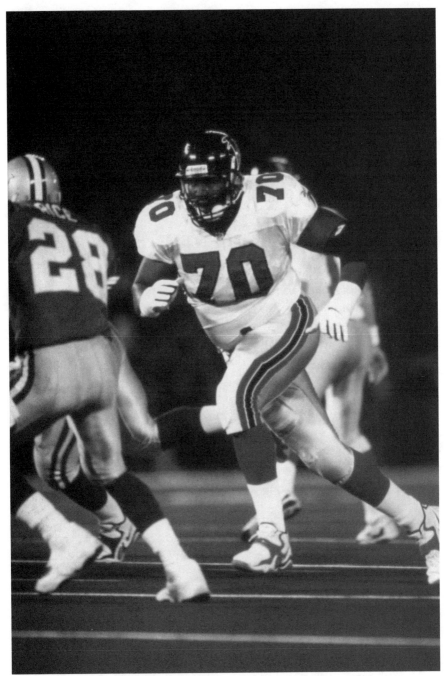

*Bob "Chi-Chi" Whitfield set the franchise record at 123 straight starts.*

"They were the old, 'Ride 'em cowboy, rock 'em, sock 'em, go-get-em cats.' They weren't running around; they were taking their hits and just getting up and saying, 'Shit. That hurt. Come on fellas, let's stick those bastards.'"

Whitfield could do without George, on the other hand.

"People didn't like Jeff. Those dudes [George and Jones] were cussing each other out, and I was loving it. There was shit like that all year. Jeff and [former safety] Kevin Ross were yelling at each other, and got into it one day. So what?"

## SOMEWHAT GENTLE GIANT

Although Whitfield is six foot five, and generally around 318 pounds, he wasn't a masher—he was more of a tactician. He went to just one Pro Bowl—as an alternate after the Super Bowl season of 1998. Many league observers long felt, with a little more work ethic, he could have gone to more Pro Bowls. He was a master of acting slow and moving fast, using deceptively quick feet and textbook hands.

"If you're looking for the water cooler, look for Bob," former kicker Morten Andersen told *The Atlanta Journal-Constitution* in 2000, as Whitfield was approaching the old franchise record of 112 consecutive starts by former center Jeff Van Note. "He'll have his leg up on it. And he's got that jog down pat."

"The prop started [in the mid-1990s] when my back started bothering me," Whitfield said. "I said, 'I'm going to put my leg up and take the pressure off my sciatic nerve.' But ... now that ... is so comfortable. That's just my stance now. My little fake speed-jog? Now that started early in life. People don't understand that practice is so much harder than games. In games, there's Gatorade. In practice, there's no Gatorade. In games, there's benches to sit down on and rest. In practice, there's no benches. In games, you can usually walk off the field. In practice, you usually got to run between fields. So I came up with this little jog-walk that from far away does look like you're running. Your arms are pumping, but you're really not moving that fast."

Reporters liked the way Whitfield talked, even if he didn't always make sense. In 1998, he was penalized for holding, a false start, and unnecessary roughness upon swinging at Troy Wilson of the Saints—all in a four-minute span. What happened?

"If I tell you, you print it up, coach reads it, and then he looks on the film, and if it's something different from what I said, I'm in big trouble," he said at the time.

Bob, you can do better than that.

"Did they ask O.J. [Simpson] what happened [after his ex-wife's murder]? What did he say? He said he was in Chicago—for all intents and purposes, I'm in Chicago. I'm going to answer just like [former president] Bill Clinton. What you asked me was do I remember what I did, and I said, 'No, I don't remember what I do recall.'"

Sit a spell with Chi-Chi … your chin may drop, and your gut may ache.

## SET IN HIS WAYS

Whitfield broke his right fibula during the 2003 season, which was going horribly for him. The team finished 5-11. Quarterback Michael Vick missed the first 11-plus games after fracturing his fibula in the preseason.

Whitfield went on injured reserve, ending his season and his career with Atlanta—he was cut late the next summer. His style didn't match that of new offensive line coach Alex Gibbs—a man somewhat notorious for disdaining oversized linemen who no longer bend their knees well.

What had changed between when Whitfield entered the league, and the 21st century version of the game?

"I never changed. I kind of stayed the same. I let the game change around me, and my approach to football changed, and I didn't change my way to it," he said in the spring of 2005.

"Back in the day, there were more Bob Whitfields and fewer Patrick Kerneys."

That was a reference to Falcons defensive end Patrick Kerney, perhaps the most diligent workout freak in team history.

"The off-season program in 1993, after my rookie year, was maybe 22 guys, sporadic show up," Whitfield said. "I don't know why they haven't just written it into contracts. They say voluntary, but everybody knows it's mandatory. Everybody is there, just about."

What else doesn't Big Bob like about the modern game?

"The softness of the game with all the quarterback protection, the helmet-to-helmet [penalties] … it was a gladiator sport when I came in," he said. "Guys were nicknamed the Hammer [like former teammate Jessie Tuggle, a middle linebacker]. Now, you barely touch a guy, and it's 15 yards. You get a guy like Chuck Smith, who's undersized, and he was good because he played hard and like a gladiator.

"You can sign for $10 million, but the next day it may be worth $2. You are sold a bill of goods. That's why I never got a Falcons tattoo. When you're under contract, and you perform better than your contract, you can't get a raise. But when you underperform, they sure can cut you quick. I hate that they try to make it a business. Always salary cappin' and stuff. This ain't no business; it's personal as hell. When times are good, you want to see smiles [from players], have Christmas parties, [have players] sign autographs for the little blind kids, but now we're talking business.

"That's the biggest contradiction, and the second one is you can't even figure out how much you're worth because you can't talk to other teams [while under contract]. You don't know how much somebody else might be willing to pay you at the time. Maybe you're more valuable to them. It should be an open market every year. Hell, it should be at any time during the season."

Who were Bob's best friends from his playing days?

"Chuck and Jam. Chuck was drafted in the same class. When we met, Chuck—he's already a Georgia guy [a native of

Athens, Georgia]—he's acclimated. I'm green; I'm from California," Whitfield said. "He's got his car, and his apartment. I'm staying in the Falcon Inn [a hotel adjacent to the old practice facility that was owned by team owner Rankin Smith and his family]. He said, 'Let me show you around.' I looked at Chuck like he was a veteran."

What was the old hotel like?

"It was bad then, but it had the best water pressure. That water would wash a layer of skin off your back. That's my best memory of the Falcon Inn. It was the best place for training camp," said the long-time left tackle who actually played right tackle early in his career. "Who wanted to be up at Furman [University, where the team moved training camp in 1999]? [Former coach] Dan [Reeves] didn't like coming out of the dining hall and seeing all the chicks in the hotel lobby between the meals. That's why we moved."

That and several financial considerations—not to mention the fact the hotel had closed.

How did Whitfield hook up with Jamal Anderson?

"Jam's always in Hollywood—with like 38 cell phones—and me and Chuck didn't like Jam at first [after he was drafted in the seventh round in 1994]. He was all cocky—cocky as hell, but he ain't playing, so we ignored him. He was behind 'Ironhead' [former running back Craig Heyward]. He's like, 'I'm from L.A., and New Jersey. Blah-blah.'

"So we go out to L.A. and play the Raiders, and he finally plays. It's short yardage and he gets cracked, and the ball popped up in the air [in a 30-17 loss]. He was so crushed. I talked to him the whole way back to Atlanta on the plane. That's how I met him."

How often do you talk to Jamal and Chuck now?

"Once every other week or so. When we talk, it's just as it was yesterday. Jamal and I just went out last month. We probably hadn't been out since the Gold Club Days [an nefarious former Atlanta strip club later closed down by the federal government as the result of a very high-profile court case that linked the establishment with organized crime]. That was the best of times, it was the worst of times."

## GLANVILLE, HAMMER, AND CARDS

Whitfield started a few businesses in Atlanta—chiefly a recording studio, Patchwerk, which has played host to the likes of megastar Usher. He has a keen business sense, and quite a memory, too.

Chi-Chi's funniest former teammate?

"Erric Pegram [1991-1994], the 'Team Wolf.' He was hairy, and he'd come out for practice with a baseball hat under his helmet," Whitfield said. "He would tell funny little stories, and he had a funny little garbled voice. No matter who tried to say something about Team Wolf, if he started telling stories about you, he'd have everybody laughing. But that was in the Glanville days."

What was different about Glanville [Head coach, 1990-1993]?

"About Glanville, we might not have won a lot of games, but it sure was fun playing football," Whitfield recalled. "We had a cast of characters. I remember one day, [former cornerback] Deion [Sanders] walks through the meeting room and calls out the black guys. He said, 'Y'all guys ain't handling your shit. You're making fools of yourselves.'

"In Glanville's days, that was our image: we were a wild and crazy team. The reason Deion said that was the young black guys—we were out in clubs and stuff."

Did the team truly live up to its 'crazy' portrayal in the press?

"Well, our last day of training camp, we'd have 'Fat Tuesday on Wednesday.' We'd party, and the rookies would pay for it. After the party was over, we'd catch buses home. They had the early bus, and the late bus. But the next day, you had to be at practice that morning. Guys would be throwing up, falling asleep, but we went to the extreme, we enjoyed ourselves."

Whitfield seemed to like the nickname Hammer, but wasn't having rapper MC Hammer on the sidelines at Glanville's invitation a bit much?

"I thought that was how the NFL was supposed to be. Hammer was on the plane with us flying to the West Coast. We'd all be gambling in the back of the plane," he said. "In the early days, a linebacker named Jesse Solomon, he could play some cards—poker and some other games. In later years, [former kicker] Jay Feely became the man to beat.

"I always thought I was pretty good, but I was always losing money. [Former fellow offensive linemen] Jamie Dukes and Houston Hoover used to cheat. You'd have six guys playing at a time—two in back standing up looking over seats, two in front looking back over their seats to the two in the middle. Dukes and Hoov sat in the same row so they could slide a card to the side. I'd tell them, 'I ain't ever playing with your cheating asses again.' But I did."

What kind of impression did Glanville leave?

"He knew his stuff, but he did some stuff I didn't like. Eric Dickerson, they bring him into camp [in a trade before the 1993 season, when he rushed just 26 times for 91 yards and Pegram rushed for 1,185]. Hall of Famer Eric Dickerson, and we had nine-on-seven, with extra defensive players, and you know what Jerry does? We go full speed [tackling included] nine-on-seven, but the defense has more players than the offense. There's two safeties unblocked. Eric got his neck damn near broken by those safeties, I think it was Scott Case and Tracey Eaton."

## FLYING AROUND

Whitfield got in some scraps, but he was not known as a fighter. He said the best player he ever worked against was Chuck Smith. Interestingly, he said the meanest player he faced was another former Falcon.

"Aundray Bruce's punk ass. He hit me with the worst bull-shit cheap shot," Whitfield recalled. "This was after he left the Falcons. When I got there, he was already gone. This was a pre-season game: the ball went downfield, and he hit me in the back of the head. He was talking shit all day."

Atlanta made Bruce, a former Auburn linebacker, the No. 1 overall pick of the 1988 draft; but he stunk it up for the Falcons, and in 1991 he joined the Raiders. Whitfield met him in a pre-season game some years later, saying this years after:

"He's just talking shit like he's a beast. I just gave him the truth; I said, 'You suck. You're a first-round bust.' I'm hip-toss-ing this m****rf***er around, and he just whacks me in the head. I'm not one to talk—it's a waste of energy. I conserve my energy. But I'm not going to just take a bunch of shit, either."

Sometimes Whitfield took up for others.

He was right in the middle of things, or on the bottom of things, in a training camp fight in 2001, when his buddy—Lord Jam—started a fray on a rainy, muddy afternoon at Furman.

"I think Dan [Reeves] intensified camp; Dan wanted it to be harder. Jam would trot through there, and nobody would hit him. He'd hit you, and you couldn't hit him back. Jamal would do that; they weren't allowed to touch him, but he'd stiff-arm them, or hit them," Whitfield said. "Dudes hated that, and they started firing on Jam. They gave him a crack, Jam got up mad, and [pushed safety Chris Hudson from behind]. Then former linebacker Jeff Kelly pushed Anderson, and a brawl was on. I came flying with some of those Malachi elbow-chops," said the aspiring pro wrestler.

It's true. Big Bob flew—at least for a moment. But after div-ing, he wrestled only air before making contact with the grass.

"I missed, and when I looked up there were two little midgets on me—DBs." he said. "Oh, Jesus, it was on. Yeah, that shit hurt. I missed, and then I got beat up by a DB [Hudson]. I was on the bottom of the pile."

Several plays later, coaches sent in reserve running back Travis Jervey, but Anderson pushed Jervey out of the way. He scored, spiked the ball, and barked at the No. 1 defense on the sideline, "I don't want to see the twos. Don't be disrespecting me with the twos."

# PLAYING PRANKS

Although hazing hasn't disappeared from the league, it is rare—which saddens Chi-Chi, who said the best prankster he played with was Pegram:

"In the early days, the Team Wolf [Pegram]. But as time started going on, the pranking started leaving. It went soft, and everybody's preaching this stuff, the coaches. [Current Falcons coach] Jim Mora did it, said, 'There's no hazing,' [before the 2004 season]. Dan [Reeves] didn't want us to haze anybody."

Yet Whitfield took his turns.

"I used to be the prankster. We'd tie the rookies up, or wake them up with a water drip. They'd wake up and think they pissed themselves. At that old Falcon Inn, we'd run a hose from the maids' quarters. They'd give us the master key.

"One night, we were getting everybody, and [center-guard] Calvin Collins was a rookie [in 1997, Reeves's first season as coach]. We were getting guys with tie-downs, the water, dragging some out to the goalposts to tape them up. Calvin called all the other guys who were getting hazed. So by the time we tried to get into his room, they put the security latch on. We were like, 'How'd they do that?' We had to get him for that.

"So we took all his football equipment. He was about to cry before practice the next day. I caved in. Another time, [linebacker] Clay Matthews was on the team, and we had a rookie linebacker. I can't remember his name, but the rookies had to go get chicken for the veterans, and he's cussing at the veterans. Clay Matthews is egging him on, saying, 'He said, 'F*** you,'' and, 'He ain't getting no f***ing chicken.' So we had to go get our own chicken.

"We got off the practice field, because back in the day we didn't have a dining hall; we had to fend for ourselves. And this mother f***er who wouldn't go get the chicken, he's eating all the chicken! After he ate all the chicken, he showered and then got dressed. He pulls his jeans on, and puts his hand in his pocket, and he got a chicken breast. In his back pocket, there were drumsticks. He had about 40 pounds of chicken in his clothes, everywhere. We even jammed chicken way down in his shoes. He got his chicken."

## CHEMISTRY MATTERS

For all the players he played with, Whitfield said the best times came when the most players were kept around by management.

"It seemed to mesh easier when you knew dudes. You know a guy best when you've been with him a long time, when you've been through shit," he said. "The best year was that Super Bowl year [1998], and the reason was it was the same crew as the year before, the same crew that started bad [1-7] and improved [to 7-9] in 1997. There were only a couple of years where everybody stayed mostly intact—'97 and '98—and that's when it worked out."

One of the key players on that 1998 team was free safety Eugene Robinson, who was arrested on the eve of Super Bowl XXXIII for soliciting an undercover female police officer in Miami.

"It wasn't a distraction for us," Whitfield said. "I found out from [rookie right tackle] Ephraim [Salaam]; he called me. Ephraim wasn't asleep yet, and he saw the news. He called me. I was watching a Super Bowl skit on *MAD-TV*. I called back and said, 'Gene didn't get arrested, this is *MAD-TV*.' He said, 'Just watch the news; you'll see.'

"It didn't show up, and that's when I called Chuck and Jamal. I said, 'Jam, find out.'

"'Baby-baby'—that's what we called 'Gene—Jamal called Baby-Baby. He [Robinson] had just won NFL Man of the Year [that morning]—his wife, kids, and everybody's in town. The night before the game—he just went to jail. You ain't getting much sleep that night."

Indeed, Robinson was up late—speaking with teammates, including his good friend, cornerback Ray Buchanan. Reeves offered counsel, too and—in an adjacent hotel suite—Reeves's wife, Pam, tried to console Robinson's wife, Gia.

Robinson was beaten by Denver wide receiver Rod Smith for an 80-yard touchdown the next night, and the Broncos repeated as Super Bowl champions with a 34-19 win over the 16-2 Falcons. Whitfield felt Robinson's arrest was not a factor in any way.

"We were out there balling," he said. "Dan brushed over that shit so fast. The only thing Dan should have done differently in my opinion was re-evaluating his [Robinson] starting. Sit him down for a play, maybe make him re-focus."

## WHAT ABOUT BOB?

Whitfield's former teammates aren't as likely to remember him for his failed flying turnbuckle maneuver in training camp or specific pranks. They'll remember how goofy he was and his wandering eye—his most distinctive physical characteristic.

"I was born with a underdeveloped right eye," he said. "The optic nerve never developed. I don't have full control of it. That's why it will cross sometimes. That's why the Creator gave me a neck—so I can turn my head."

When asked who was the funniest Falcon he'd ever known, he maintained his humility.

"It'd have to be me," said the new-age gangster who often played by his own rules rather than those of his society. "I hate to toot my own whistle, but shit—I'm a funny guy. I say the shit nobody else is going to say. I'm saying the shit everybody is thinking."

Another Bob, former teammate Bob Christian—a very good fullback from 1997-2002—agreed.

"Just don't think too hard in trying to understand everything Whitfield says and you'll be fine," said little Bob. "Some of it just won't add up. A lot of it's not meant to make sense, I think," said Christian, a voluminous speaker in his own right. "That's Bob—you laugh at him, enjoy it, and keep moving."

# CHAPTER TWELVE

# Shot Down

To a man, everybody felt differently the second time around. When the Falcons got another shot at the Cowboys in the playoffs—two years after their failed visit to Texas Stadium—the proverbial shoe was on the other foot.

The Falcons were expected to win, and the oddsmakers agreed.

"Playing the Cowboys here at home, we were very confident they couldn't stop our offense," said former center Jeff Van Note, looking back more than 24 years to the January 4, 1981 meeting in Atlanta-Fulton County Stadium with the perennial NFC power.

Van Note and his teammates were giddy when they beat the Eagles in a home playoff game in 1978, after earning a wildcard berth. Their game the next week at Dallas was a bonus of sorts, which is not to say that losing 27-20 after leading 20-13 didn't hurt like hell.

But that team was in the playoffs for the first time in its history, and the Cowboys, at that time, were 11 months removed from a Super Bowl Championship. Dallas was supposed to win.

In the 1980 season, the Falcons were the power. In 1979, things fell apart in many ways, although fullback William Andrews's rookie season was a sign of things to come, as Atlanta went 6-10.

A year later, in 1980, it was on. Andrews, a fresh face from Thomasville, Georgia via Auburn, pounded and gouged his way for 1,308 rushing yards with a whopping 4.9-yard average. Bartkowski put it all together, throwing for 3,544 yards with 31 touchdowns and 16 interceptions. Atlanta put up 405 points, and four receivers caught at least six touchdown passes—tight end Junior Miller caught nine, wide receivers Wallace Francis and Alfred Jackson seven each, and Alfred Jenkins six.

Even Tom Landry, veteran of five Super Bowl appearances as the head coach in Dallas, noticed, saying in the final month of the season, "I would say Atlanta, based on its performance over the year, should be in the favorite's role."

A nine-game winning streak ended in the regular-season finale, with a 20-17 overtime loss to the Rams, but the Falcons captured their first division title, winning the NFC West with a 12-4 mark. Leeman Bennett was named NFC Coach of the Year, and all was well as Atlanta sat home during a bye. The Cowboys, a wildcard team, thrashed the Rams 34-13 to earn a trip to Atlanta.

Atlanta was abuzz, and players were pumped, too. Defensive end Jeff Merrow had said: "I think we should be America's Team. People enjoy watching us."

Before the second-round playoff game, a headline in *The Atlanta Journal* read, "Falcons' vow: We Won't Choke Against Cowboys" the day of the game.

However, that's exactly what happened—the Falcons blew it.

*On what he called "the most disappointing day ever for us," Bartkowski completed 25 of 39 passes for 322 yards.*

Van Note jogged his memory decades later. He probably wishes he could forget some things. He remembered Bartkowski going bananas, which he did—completing 18 of 33 passes for 320 yards with one interception and two touchdowns.

"They wanted to take William away," the former center said, explaining that the Cowboys stacked the line of scrimmage to limit Atlanta to 86 rushing yards, 43 by Andrews, and 43 by Lynn Cain. "That was their game plan."

It worked, but Bartkowski was rolling. At halftime—when the Falcons led 17-10—Dallas president Tex Schramm bumped into Falcons owner Rankin Smith and said, "Did you know that in the playoffs so far, every team that has been behind has won?"

Smith later reported: "That really pissed me off. I said, 'Kiss my ass.'"

Atlanta pushed the lead to 24-10 in the third quarter. Later linebacker Joel Williams tracked down Dallas running back Preston Pearson on a screen pass and poked the ball loose from behind, Atlanta recovered. A Tim Mazzetti field goal gave Atlanta a 27-17 lead. Just 6:37 remained in the game, and the Cowboys' comeback master, quarterback Roger Staubach, was in a blazer helping out as a broadcaster for CBS. He'd retired after the 1979 season.

That left quarterback/punter Danny White to run the Cowboys' show—and run it he did, hitting four passes in a six-play, 62-yard drive. The last, a 14-yarder to wide receiver Drew Pearson, pulled the Cowboys to within 27-24 with 3:40 remaining.

The stadium tensed, remembering what happened two years earlier, but these weren't the same Falcons. Bartkowski and the boys had been wonderful in the second half all season, outscoring opponents 231-120.

Many fans in the stands also supported the University of Georgia, which just days earlier had won the national championship behind freshman running back Herschel Walker. The Bulldogs that year invoked a mantra; calling it "Dooley's Law" in honor of head coach Vince Dooley. It went like this: Whatever can go right, will.

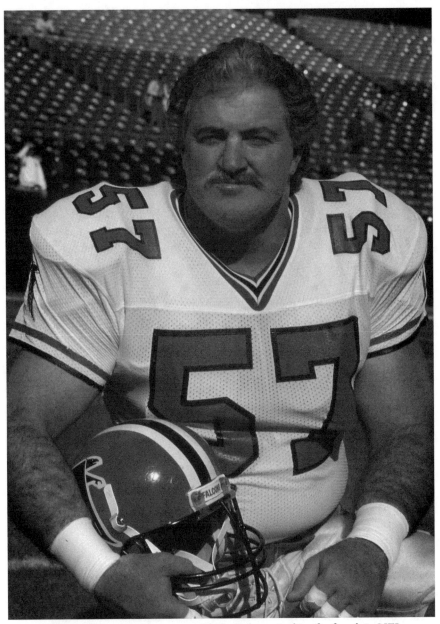

*Center Jeff Van Note's 18 years with the Falcons ties him for fourth in NFL history for service with one team. His six Pro Bowls tied former defensive end Claude Humphrey for most in franchise history. He's first in consecutive games played (155) and second in games played (246), games started (225), and consecutive starts (112) for the Falcons.*

Soon, though, fate, the football gods, or the dexterity of Dallas defensive end Ed "Too Tall" Jones intervened. Whatever it was, something conspired against the Falcons. Murphy's law—Whatever can go wrong, will—draped the Birds.

Trying to run the clock, the Falcons faced third-and-three. Jones, from his left end spot, jumped offsides. He did not touch an Atlanta blocker, however, which would've prompted an encroachment penalty, a five-yard mark-off, and an Atlanta first down. Jones's momentum wouldn't allow him to back straight up, although he retreated to his side of the line of scrimmage.

He went the way he was leaning—to his right—parallel with the line of scrimmage. Almost a quarter century after the fact, Van Note lamented his role—or non-role—in that one play. "Too Tall was coming down the line, and I should have snapped the ball [while Jones was across the line, which also would've triggered the penalty call], but in Leeman's system, he didn't want to do that. I should've done it anyway."

Jones ran right into a sweep to Atlanta's left by Cain—no gain—plenty of pain. "He was nearly offsides, and goes right down the line and falls into the hole where we're running the play," said Bennett, who as recently as 2004 still helped with a local radio show (not on the flagship station) in Atlanta. "Who knows what would've happened if he hadn't done that?"

What happened was Atlanta punted. It all remains fresh in Van Note's mind.

"I think when we were up 10 with seven minutes left, we just went very conservative, and there were a couple of key plays," he said. "We went with the run, and they were trying to take the run away. Danny White got hot. It was the highest point of the Falcons' existence, and it became the lowest. Bart had a big night, and I think he could've thrown at will."

Cowboys safety Charlie Waters confirmed as much after the game. "We might have played the best team in the NFL today," he said. "I think the Falcons got a little bit scared near the end. It was like they were saying, 'Oh, no, Dallas has been through this so many times … they've won so many of these … they're going to do it again."

Bartkowski added: "I thought if we made two first downs, we'd win. We didn't even make one."

Atlanta still led, but now Danny White was rolling. The Cowboys got the ball back at their 30-yard line with 1:48 left.

Although Atlanta defensive coordinator Jerry Glanville had favored the blitz much of the year, he hadn't used it as often through the first three quarters as the Cowboys short-circuited the Falcons' defense frequently with a series of screen passes.

"They were running the option screen, and it was hard to drop back on coverage deep and then sprint out on the screen while you're trying to play the run, too," said former linebacker Fulton Kuykendall. "In that situation, we only had two men rushing."

Atlanta returned to the blitz on the Cowboys' last possession. "They picked it up well, like they knew what we were going to do," said defensive tackle Don Smith. "That meant we had a lot of man coverage, which hurt us."

On the sideline, Jenkins was hurting inside—almost sick to his stomach. He'd caught four passes for 155 yards, including a 60-yard touchdown pass early in the game. That might've been a bad sign. In 10 previous career games in which he had at least 100 receiving yards, the Falcons lost eight.

"I'm superstitious," he said later. "It just wasn't a good omen. It happens every time. Every time I have a big game, we lose. If that's the way it's going to be, then I guess I'd rather never have a big game."

Again, the Cowboys ran six plays, and White completed four passes. One of his incompletions went through the hands of Atlanta rookie cornerback Kenny Johnson—a potential game-clinching play wrenchingly wasted.

Once the Cowboys reached the Falcons' 23-yard line, White sensed a blitz. He—like Bartkowski—had a huge day, completing 25 of 39 passes for 322 yards. He chose to audible, knowing the Falcons were going to throw man-to-man coverage at Dallas; he wanted Drew Pearson one-on-one with cornerback Rolland Lawrence.

The blitz worked to a degree, as White was flushed out of the pocket to his right. He tossed a flutter ball, and Pearson ran under it for a touchdown—White's third versus one interception.

Atlanta safety Tom Pridemore fell to his knees after Pearson's go-ahead score, in disbelief. "You're just at a loss for words," he said later. "I don't think anybody here is ready to go home. We had a 10-point lead with six minutes to go. I can't believe it happened."

Dallas missed the PAT after a poor snap, but it didn't matter.

"They did get more conservative offensively late in the game," White said afterward, "opening a seam for us to crack."

The Falcons, who got the ball back with 42 seconds left, could hardly believe they had cracked. The best season in franchise history was over four plays later, as Atlanta couldn't muster a first down or move into Mazzetti's range. Bartkowski completed a 17-yard pass to Francis, but the Falcons needed 19 yards due to an earlier sack. Dallas had outscored Atlanta 20-3 in the final quarter.

"When you sweat, and you bleed, and work like we have since last August, it shouldn't end this way," Bartkowski said. "I thought before the game that we would score 27 or more points and we did ... but we lost. This is the most disappointing day ever for us."

Francis echoed that thought. "I don't know how we lost, or why we lost," he said. "It really hasn't dawned on me yet that we lost."

Bennett was as dumbfounded as anybody was. "Playing in Atlanta the last few years, you get to know that all it takes is one second to get off one play," the coach said. "You have to prepare yourself for both sides of that. I guess Danny White's killed us twice now in the playoffs."

White had just led the Cowboys to the first of three consecutive NFC Championship games (they'd lose all three—to the Eagles, 49ers and Redskins respectively).

"Today," Dallas running back Tony Dorsett said, "we should have ended all the questions about this team and Roger Staubach. I don't think anyone should ever ask again if we could win in the pressure game without Roger. Case closed."

Even Staubach gave a ringing endorsement of his successor on CBS. "That was one of the greatest comebacks in the history of the Dallas Cowboys," he said. "No quarterback could have done a better job than Danny White did. No one."

## SINKING LIKE A ROCK

Soon after the Cowboys beat the Falcons, Landry said: "If their program keeps going in the direction it's going, they'll be a Super Bowl team. It's a matter of being in big games and winning them, but I know the Falcons are a much better football team than when we last played them."

That endorsement was hollow. It didn't happen the way it was supposed to—although they won their first three games, the Falcons were 7-9 in 1981. Atlanta lost six games by three points or less.

When former Rams linebacker Jack "Hacksaw" Reynolds arrived at media day for the Super Bowl after that season, when he was playing for the 49ers, he said: "I think the two best teams are here [at the Super Bowl], but the Atlanta Falcons had the personnel to make it. They just did so many stupid things."

It was little better in 1982, when the season saw seven games canceled by a player strike. The Falcons were 5-4, made the playoffs, but lost 30-24 at Minnesota. Owner Rankin Smith said a couple days later that he had "no plans to fire anybody."

Soon after that, Bennett walked into the owner's office with a wish list for the 1983 season, some suggestions for player moves and so forth. Smith never did review the list—he fired him, leaving the now former coach to speak of betrayal and the feeling of being used. Bennett boasted a 47-44 record in six seasons, along with the team's only three playoff appearances. All previous Atlanta coaches had combined for a record of just 50-100-4.

*Constitution* columnist Jesse Outlar wrote:

*"Rankin Smith Sr. remarked earlier in the week that he was-
n't planning to fire anybody, but he has never been overly reliable
in matters pertaining to his Atlanta Falcons, a team that has won
only one playoff game in 17 seasons in the National Football
League."*

Former coach Norm Van Brocklin threw in his two cents,
saying: "It seems a little unfair to me. They're a better football
team than they played this year, but they had extenuating circumstances—similar to the circumstances I had in 1974 with a
darn strike."

There were media reports that general manager Tom Braatz
suggested to Smith that a coaching change was needed, but
Braatz angrily denied that a couple days later.

Smith simply said: "We won the Western Division championship in 1980, and we set off in a period of euphoria. We
thought this team had arrived. For whatever reason, it had not
arrived. And it appeared to the organization, and, reluctantly, to
me, that we were going backward rather than forward."

The start of the Falcons' darkest age was at hand.

## THREE PLAYERS DIE

It's hard to imagine an NFL team going through a worse
stretch than the Falcons in the eight years after Bennett was
dismissed.

Dan Henning earned considerable acclaim in the 1982 season as offensive coordinator of the world-champion Redskins,
and Smith hired him the day after the Super Bowl.

Atlanta went 7-9 in his first season, as Andrews set a franchise record with 1,567 rushing yards, and Bartkowski completed 63.4 percent of his passes while throwing just five interceptions in 432 pass attempts. Yet, the defense and special teams
didn't hold up their end of the deal.

Henning and the Falcons' mostly dead decade went downhill from there with records of 4-12 (after Andrews suffered a

season-ending knee injury in a preseason practice) in 1984, 4-12 in 1985, and 7-8-1 (after starts of 4-0 and 5-1-1 after Bartkowski signed with the Rams) in 1986. Soon thereafter, Henning was gone as well.

Dick Vermeil, the former Eagles coach, declined Smith's offer to coach the team, instead remaining as an announcer.

Ultimately, Marion Campbell, who'd served as the Eagles' defensive coordinator and then head coach after Vermeil stepped down, was hired first as defensive coordinator and then bumped up to head coach early in 1987—about a month after Henning had been fired—for an encore. It was an unsuccessful return, beginning with a 3-12 record in the strike-shortened 1987 season, and a mark of 5-11 in 1988.

The records paled in comparison to the pall cast over the organization with the cocaine overdose death of defensive back David Croudip on October 10, 1988.

Before the 1989 draft, the Falcons traded their all-time leading rusher, Gerald Riggs (who'd replaced the injured Andrews in 1984), to the Redskins for two draft choices. Campbell resigned that autumn after going 3-9, ending what might've been the most dreadful tour of duty by an Atlanta head coach, pocked horribly by the death of not one, but two players.

Shortly before Campbell surrendered, rookie offensive tackle Ralph Norwood, selected with one of the picks gained in the Riggs trade (running back Steve Broussard, selected in the first round in 1990, was the other), died in a one-car accident in 1989. He went off the road and hit a tree a few miles from the team facility after celebrating an early Thanksgiving with some teammates.

Campbell soon left only a vapid statement behind, departing with a career NFL record of 34-80-1 as a head coach, and a mark of 17-51 in two stints with Atlanta.

Finding another head coach was again difficult. Offensive line coach Jim Hanifan grudgingly accepted the interim position. There were unconfirmed stories that he agreed only after team vice president Taylor Smith and others had convinced him after discussions with NFL officials any losses incurred would not go on Hanifan's permanent record, but rather on Campbell's.

As the Falcons went 0-4 to finish the 1989 season (each game landing on Hanifan's record after all), it got no better.

Hanifan at least made things interesting and succeeded to a point. "At the end of Hanny's first practice, he holds up dynamite, and I'm like, 'What's he going to do? Blow up the team?' They probably deserved it," recalled former *Journal-Constitution* sportswriter Len Pasquarelli, who was in his first year on the beat.

"It was dummy dynamite, and he had everybody touch them, and said, 'This is what we're going to do. We're going to blow up Sunday.' They actually played well, led 10-6, but lost [23-10] to the [Super Bowl champion] 49ers."

Before the next game at Minnesota, Hanifan had three disarmed grenades, which, like the fake dynamite, he'd borrowed from his cousin—a retired army colonel. One was for the offense, one was for defense, and one was for special teams. They didn't work, either.

Finally, a vintage World War II-era bomb showed up in the lobby of team headquarters. Painted red and black, it carried a sign that read, "No more Mr. Nice Guys."

Pasquarelli wrote that an anonymous player said, "Jim's going to keep doing this until we get the point. Hell, if we lose to Washington on Sunday, he's liable to show up for that last game [against Detroit] with something nuclear."

The bomb bombed, too. The Falcons lost 31-30 to the Redskins.

The Falcons lost again, and matters grew far more grave a day later in what was, unquestionably, the worst year in franchise history.

Another player died.

Reserve tight end Brad Beckman was killed in a three-vehicle accident. He and former teammate Jeff Modesitt, who'd been released months earlier by the Falcons, were on their way

*The hiring of Jerry Glanville as head coach brought extra energy to the Falsons, closing the darkest period in franchise history.*

home at around 4 a.m. on I-85 in Gwinnett County when
Modesitt rear-ended another vehicle in icy conditions.

When Modesitt was out of the vehicle checking damage, a
tractor-trailer smashed into the car, killing Beckman instantly.

That raised to five the number of Falcons players to die of
unnatural causes while under contract—including linebacker
Andy Spivey who died after a traffic accident following the
1978 season, and running back Ron Rector, who died in a
motorcycle accident outside Columbus, Ohio, in the summer
of 1968.

"You hesitate to say it, but it's like there's a black cloud
hanging over this team, and it won't go away," club president
Rankin Smith Jr. told Pasquarelli.

The season finale dumped more salt in the wounds. Just
7,792 fans showed up for a cold, gray Christmas Eve game
against the Lions, who won 31-24 behind rookie running back
Barry Sanders. The parking lots were almost empty before the
game.

"It's the first time in my life I ever walked up to a stadium,
and said, 'Am I in the right city? Is this game being played in
Detroit?'" Pasquarelli said almost 16 years later. "I actually
paused for a nanosecond, and said, 'OK, Lenny, did you screw
this up?'

"The crazy part about the season was the team just quit on
Marion Campbell. I've never seen a more limp effort out of an
NFL team in 25 years covering the NFL. Halfway through the
season, nobody wanted to be there," said Pasquarelli, who has
gone on to cover the NFL for ESPN.com. "It was a team just
biding time, waiting for the season to be over. It's hard to put
into words how bad that season was."

## HAM-HANDED HANDOFF

From Bennett's firing after the 1982 season to the hiring of
former Oilers coach Jerry Glanville early in 1990, Atlanta
had a record of 38-77-1—underachieving a paltry winning per-
centage of .332.

They went most of the 1980s (and most of the 1990s) without a general manager and still didn't have one. But Glanville, the team's former defensive coordinator during the semi-glory days of the Bennett era, came in spouting all kinds of inspiration. He was a breath of air—lots of it actually—though not everyone would say it was fresh.

Still, the Falcons couldn't turn a page in their history without it catching fire.

Just weeks after Glanville was hired, the "black cloud" choked Rankin Smith Jr., who was run off as team president, to be succeeded by his younger brother, Taylor.

The move was triggered when the eldest of Rankin Smith Sr.'s five children was hit with a paternity suit in connection with two illegitimate children. Smith Jr. never disputed fathering the children, and in fact had previously signed an agreement to support them and pay for their education. There were problems with his payments, however, and he was sued.

Smith Jr.'s wife filed for divorce. Soon after leaving the Falcons, he divested his interest in the team, and was rarely seen publicly over the final 13 years before Arthur Blank bought the team.

Fittingly—one might say—team officials soon announced that they were changing their primary color from red to black.

# CHAPTER THIRTEEN

# Remember Them?

Although many black holes exist in the vast expanse of space, Atlanta for many years seemed to be the only one present in the NFL universe.

The Falcons, in their first 39 seasons, were below .500 in 27 and at .500 in two. They made the playoffs eight times in those ten remaining seasons—including two of three since Arthur Blank bought the team in early 2002.

A spring 2005 trip to the Atlanta-Fulton Public Library proved that the Falcons still had not escaped their ignominious past. Entering "Atlanta Falcons" into a search engine yielded just eight results in the metro area's biggest library. Some were not even in the main library, but rather in satellite outposts around town.

Six of the eight were children's books, generally 32 pages long—done by a company in Minnesota. The other two were books about Brett Favre and Deion Sanders, whom long-time Falcons fans know left town long before leaving the NFL.

Call it the mark of the NFL's black bird.

Michael Vick, Blank, and Mora are conspiring to change this, of course. It should be said there are other books out there that pertain to the Falcons, or some of their players. That includes a few of several books by former Atlanta defensive lineman-turned-author/broadcaster Tim Green (some of which are in the AFP Library, although they didn't show up in that search because the Falcons are not the primary subject).

One gets the idea. Obscurity, thy name is Falcons. Favre and Sanders will never qualify as obscure. And although both began their careers in Atlanta, neither will enter the Hall of Fame as Falcons, and both will be cast in bronze in Canton, Ohio—where no Falcon's bust currently resides.

At least Sanders flashed across the Atlanta landscape, even if merely as a shooting star, before opting to play for San Francisco in 1994, then much more money to play for Dallas and Washington. A stint in a CBS broadcast booth was followed with a post-retirement stint as a nickel back in Baltimore. Before all that, he was All-Pro in three of his five Atlanta campaigns.

One must also consider a baseball career that watered down his impact in Atlanta, though not his caliber of play. In that way, he was amazing. The residue left in the form of awkward moments, words and deeds, however, was also great.

Favre threw five passes for the Falcons, completing two—to opponents.

Yet it was no wonder former Falcons president Taylor Smith eventually wanted to puke over the idea of trading Favre to the Packers on February 10, 1992—after one season as Atlanta's No. 3 signal caller. In Green Bay, he won three NFL MVP awards.

Favre's trade didn't seem like a big deal back then. Chris Miller was entrenched as Atlanta's quarterback in 1991—Jerry Glanville's second season as head coach—putting up statistics

*Admittedly footloose in his younger days, former Falcons quarterback Brett Favre believes part of the reason he was traded from Atlanta had to do with the fact that he let his hair down a little too much as a rookie to suit former coach Jerry Glanville.*

that led his team to the playoffs and Miller, then 26, to his only Pro Bowl.

Billy Joe Tolliver—not exactly a superstar in training but a more than serviceable player at age 25—was No. 2. That left Favre, a second-round draft pick in 1991 out of Southern Mississippi, with time on his hands as a rookie.

He spent that idle time somewhat wildly, hitting the city's Buckhead bar district with some regularity—although he mildly disputed his reputation as a party king.

Although some time had to pass before a formal debate arose, there were differing tales on whose idea it was to ship Favre north for a first-round pick. Atlanta ended up using that pick to select running back Tony Smith No. 17 overall. He played from 1992-1994, gaining 329 yards with two touchdowns on 87 carries as a rookie. He never carried the ball for Atlanta again.

Whether Favre's exit was Glanville's decision or that of Vice President of Player Personnel Ken Herock, remains uncertain. The jury remains hung as permutations of the story continue to surface. Those who have their opinions, it should be noted, do not seem about to change them. Favre said a couple years after the trade that he had understood well its design.

"I was a young guy, sitting on the bench for the first time in my life … what was I going to do, just feel sorry for myself?" Favre told the *Journal-Constitution* in 1994 while admitting that he had a few beers as a rookie. "Look, I'd always said that when I got the chance to play, when I became a starter, I'd cut back on the partying and all. And that's what I've done [in Green Bay], and I would have [done it] there, too, under the same circumstances. Kenny was the guy who drafted me and fought for me, and I'm pretty sure it was Jerry who said, 'Get him out of here.' But things have worked out for the best."

Easy for him to say.

Favre wasn't shocked when the *Journal-Constitution*'s Len Pasquarelli reached him at his parents' home in Kiln, Mississippi, for his reaction to the trade.

"Having three young guys like that, and only one of us being completely happy as the starter, I knew it was going to happen; I just had a feeling," Favre said. "I'm a little shocked, but not totally. The bad part is, I'm leaving a lot of friends and a brand-new house behind. The good part is, I'm going to have a chance to play pretty quickly. The way they've talked, I can be the man up there.

"The big plus is, it's going to be a new offense for everyone, [Don] Majkowski, [Mike] Tomczak, all those guys up there. We'll all have to learn it together, so it's not like I'm going into a situation where I'm blindfolded and everyone else has 20/20 vision, you know? There's a lot of upside to this, I guess."

There was no guesswork to be done. In the third game of 1992, Majkowski [who eventually settled in Atlanta] injured his left ankle. Favre took over, and the Wally Pipp/Lou Gehrig story had an instant NFL equivalent.

The young gunslinger, working in a new offense installed by first-year head coach Mike Holmgren (whom the Falcons considered but never interviewed to be their head coach in 1990, when they hired Glanville) rallied the Packers to a 24-23 victory over the Bengals. The winning 35-yard pass came with 13 seconds left—landing in the hands of another former Falcon, wide receiver Kitrick Taylor.

"It gave me chills," Favre said afterward. "It felt [upon entering the game] like I had just taken a laxative. I was shaking all over. Thank goodness I managed to hold it in until the whole thing was over with."

The Falcons' former president could relate.

A few days before Favre and the defending world champion Packers took on the Broncos in Super Bowl XXXII, both men were asked to look back on the trade.

"Really, it wasn't like [the Falcons] collapsed [after he was traded], because they were always kind of flat line anyway, with maybe a peak here and there," Favre said. "But our guys took off from that point. I mean: the curve is still going up. Still, who's to say Atlanta would not have done the same thing, you know? Just where might they be right now?"

*Brett Favre won three NFL MVP awards while playing for the Packers, but he attempted just five passes in his single season with the Falcons. The former second-round draft choice did not complete any and threw two interceptions in 1991.*

From the time of the trade up to that Super Bowl—after the 1997 season—the Packers amassed a record of 73-35 (.676), went to the playoffs five times, and won three straight division titles, two NFC titles, and a Super Bowl. Favre at that point had started 105 straight games, a streak still intact at an NFL-record 205 consecutive regular season games heading into the 2005 season.

The Falcons from 1992-1997 were 39-58 (.402), with one playoff berth (and a 37-20 loss at Green Bay on New Year's Eve, 1995), and tried seven different starting quarterbacks.

"That is," Favre said, "a damned big difference, ain't it?"

No doubt. Smith's review of the trade was gut-wrenching as Favre was fresh off his third straight MVP.

"Sure, it's something you agonize over," he told the *Journal-Constitution*. "He's a special player and a special person, so it's something that will bother you forever. The way Brett plays the game, with so much fun and natural [charisma], he could have changed any franchise. You know, it makes you want to throw up."

## PRIME TIME HGH MAINTENENCE

By the end of the 1993 season, which was the last of Glanville's four as head coach, Smith had learned well the frequent absence of joy that accompanied the team's presidency.

Beyond making the playoffs in 1991—Glanville's second season—Atlanta tolerated the colorful head coach's antics on and off the field as he put together a combined record of 28-38, including a stirring playoff win at New Orleans in 1991. The show was interesting at times, but its star performer wore down Smith.

Sanders, the No. 5 overall pick of the 1989 draft, was actually something of a part-time cornerback and return man, splitting time between the Falcons and baseball's Braves. For the fuzzy memories of long-time Atlanta fans who lament the team letting him "get away" in 1994 (he signed a one-year deal with the 49ers), a history lesson is in order.

*Deion Sanders was an outstanding cornerback and a decent baseball player. Most objective observers would say he was the most talented Falcon of all time.*

For all his brilliance on the field and oft-magnetic person-ality, Deion was difficult to accommodate. He changed his mind frequently on whether he was going to play baseball or football full time, and griped at times about the business meth-ods of Atlanta's front office. Perhaps his comments had merit, but making them so public lacked that honor.

Late in the summer of 1992, when he was absent from training camp yet again while playing baseball, Sanders didn't like the vibe he was getting from the Falcons.

"The thing is, I'm not worried about their damned front office," he told the *Journal-Constitution*. "They're not out on the field. I've got 46 teammates who want to win and be successful. And that's what I want, too. That's why I won't just say the hell with them. Brian Jordan [the former Falcons strong safety who signed a baseball-only contract with St. Louis], he said the hell with them, but he made a bad business decision."

In 1993 alone, Sanders went back and forth a few times on whether he would play football at all once his Atlanta contract expired after that season.

"Maybe it's time to put all my focus on baseball and give that everything I've got so that I really have a great season," he said after a late-season loss to the Bengals. "The people around here ... they've taken away some of my love for the game with the things they've done this year."

A month earlier, before negotiations designed (failingly) to extend his soon-to-expire contract took a turn for the worse, he said: "I'm happy, the Falcons have taken care of me. I want to be a Falcon for the rest of my life," in a conference call with reporters from out of town.

His vacillations between football and baseball were as annu-ally dependable as the blooming of Azalea shrubs in Georgia.

## A REAL JETSETTER

It was impossible to question Sanders's commitment—whatever sport he was playing. He played to win, period, and usually played football brilliantly. Some consider him the best cover-cornerback in NFL history, although a certain segment of the media loved to lampoon his tentative tackling style. He also was a breathtaking return man, with speed to spare.

There was no outrunning the awkward feeling, though, when he commuted back and forth between the postseason Braves and the Falcons in the 1992 season.

He struck out in his only at-bat in Game 4 of the National League Championship Series on a Saturday night in Pittsburgh. Then he hopped on a charter plane to Miami, and played well for the Falcons on Sunday afternoon against the Dolphins, catching a nine-yard screen pass in addition to duties as a cornerback and return man.

That night, he sat the bench as a reserve for the Braves back in Pittsburgh.

"He looks like a piece of you-know-what warmed over," said former Falcons wide receiver Andre Rison, at one time a close friend of Sanders. "But this is something Deion wanted to do, and he'd set his mind to it. How many chances do you get to put yourself in the record books like this one?"

## STIRRING IT UP

Sanders did not once in five seasons with Atlanta report to training camp on time, and he missed a vast majority of all possible training camp time in that span either because of a contract holdout (as a rookie) or baseball.

In the summer of 1993, when he was one of four prominent veterans—including star linebacker Jessie Tuggle, stalwart offensive tackle Chris Hinton, and four-time Pro Bowler Rison—absent from training camp, he was the only one not fined.

Years earlier, Glanville shelved his rule stating that players wouldn't play in games unless they practiced—in order to accommodate Sanders when he rushed to the Falcons from his baseball duties.

Yet, as Tuggle, Hinton, and Rison incurred more that $20,000 each in fines for their insubordinations, the fact Sanders wasn't being fined wrinkled feathers. There seemed to be a double standard at play.

"I don't think there's any question that [the Falcons] selectively pick and choose who to punish and how," said Hinton's agent, Ray Anderson, who coincidentally was hired as the team's chief administrative officer (and contract negotiator) in 2002.

Dr. Charles Tucker, Rison's agent, felt much the same way. "Nothing against Deion, but I don't get it," he said. "He has a contract, so how is that different from these guys?"

In November of 1993, his final season with Atlanta (and in the same conversation in which he said he wanted to spend the rest of his career with the Falcons) Sanders dropped this: "Well, I've had some contract disputes, which every black man has. Who do you see holding out all the time? Who do you always see fighting for money? You see a lot of the 'brothers' having to fight for more."

Again, Sanders's will to win was never questioned, but he made it clear that he felt he wasn't cut enough slack at times in his dual career, and not just with the Falcons. At times, he expressed irritation with the Braves as well, although not as rancorously or as often.

Yet he always played hard. Many former teammates and team observers said he practiced as intensely as any player.

One thing was indisputable: Sanders was impossible to miss. He stood out, with his skill set, and the way he went about his business.

His first return to the Georgia Dome after leaving the Falcons was no different. Traded from the Braves to the Reds in 1994, he then joined the 49ers with a contract whose bonus structure was so unusual it had to be approved by NFL commissioner Paul Tagliabue.

He went on to win a Super Bowl ring that season, and along the way, on October 16, he visited his old home, throwing fists in a mid-field fight with Rison—and one whale of a haymaker, a 93-yard interception return of a Jeff George pass.

Nobody who was at the 49ers' 42-3 win, or watched it on TV, will forget the sight of Sanders strutting the final 50 yards, yapping at the Falcons' sideline while high-stepping as only he could.

"I've got one thing to say: This is my house," he shouted in the locker room. "I built this, and this is my house. I don't care if I'm with the Falcons or not. This is my house, and it will always be my house."

This prompted *Journal* columnist Furman Bisher to write, "Next thing you know, he'll be telling us he was born in a stable and cradled in a manger."

About the second-quarter fight, which began when somebody accidentally stuck a finger in the other player's eye, 49ers safety Toi Cook said, it was "the flurry in a hurry."

Rison later said that Sanders fought with intent. "I've never played dirty in my life," Sanders retorted. "I'm sorry it happened. It's unfortunate. I've got respect for Andre Rison. I love the man on and off the field," although their friendship had reportedly soured some time before that game.

Sanders—who once gained national attention for dumping a bucket of water on broadcaster Tim McCarver's head after an emotional postseason baseball win as payback for negative comments McCarver had made about him on the air—left Atlanta with quite the scrapbook of memories.

He once threatened to beat up a *Journal-Constitution* writer and, at times, seemed convinced that nearly everyone in the media was out to get him.

As great a football player as he was, Sanders was just as adept at letting his feelings be known in terms that trampled decorum—even when his thoughts had noble foundations, like his criticism of team officials for letting top-notch players get away.

His Atlanta legacy would be incomplete, some would say, without calling this into memory alongside his many dazzling plays and unrequited competitive spirit.

Bisher penned this lead the day after Deion's first game back in Atlanta:

*"If Senator Joe McCarthy were alive today, he'd have Deion Sanders investigated. He would consider him a national menace."*

# CHAPTER FOURTEEN

# Through Thick and Thin

Joe Curtis had his butt beat on Bourbon Street for being a Falcons fan, a most rude punishment for being the top supporter of a team that hasn't always been easy to support. Especially since he was pushing 81 years of age at the time.

"The Colonel," as the retired Air Force pilot is known to most of the Falcons fans and team officials who know him (and many do), claims to have attended every Atlanta home game—373 of them, he says—since the team opened for business in 1966, and 142 away games as well. It is believed he was the only fan, not counting the wives of players and coaches, to make the trip to Tokyo in the summer of 2000, when Atlanta played Dallas in an exhibition game.

The man's a bonafide zealot, and his love affair has won him considerable pain and suffering. It drew his blood, too, when his unwavering practice of wearing Falcons gear on road trips helped land him in a New Orleans hospital.

Curtis, who lives about 80 miles south of Atlanta near the Warner Robins Air Force Base he retired from in 1971, was making his usual rounds the night before a 1999 game with the Falcons' No. 1 rival, the Saints.

Joe's been around the Falcons in all kinds of social situations and can make the rounds with the best of them, some long-time Atlanta coaches and fans will tell you. However, bread didn't break well that night.

Some fans have said Curtis was mugged or rolled while hitting clubs. Not true, he said.

"I used to always go to [former Saints and Falcons kicker] Morten Andersen's bar down there," Curtis said. "I used to go by and take some friends before going to The Old Absinthe House [on Bourbon Street]. I made the mistake of going to this place by myself."

Curtis had plenty of company; they just happened to be the wrong kind of people—Saints fans. "There were No. 34 Ricky Williams jerseys all over the place in there," he said.

"I should have turned around right then, and minded my business. But I said, 'I'll just have one beer.' Naturally, I have my Falcons gear on, and these guys start giving me a hard time. This guy says, 'Dan Reeves is the worst coach in the NFL,' and he's just going on something awful.

"Knowing Dan Reeves as well as I did, it was obvious I was going to have trouble getting out of there. I tried maneuvering, and finally just hauled off and hit this one guy in the mouth, and knocked a few teeth out, and two other guys jumped on me, and we're rolling around."

Curtis grew up in northern Indiana listening to "Bears and Cubbies games on an old Philco radio," and said he played football and basketball at Valparaiso some six-plus decades ago. Generally, he moves better than you'd expect of an octagenarian, but just a little. Soon, however, he said he was scooting around in a hurry.

"I heard people saying either, 'Call the cops,' or 'The cops are coming.' I knew right where I was, rolled out of there, ran out, and ran down the alley. I went to The Old Absinthe House and met Joe D [special teams coach Joe DeCamillis]—one of my favorite coaches."

DeCamillis had seen Curtis in various states of disrepair, but this time The Colonel was truly a mess.

"In this melee, I head-butted a guy, and busted my glasses, and was bleeding like a stuck pig over the eye," Curtis said. "The team's old marketing guy [Rob Jackson] took me to the hospital."

## UNDYING LOVE

Most would say that a man who's bought eight to 10 season tickets for each Falcons game over four decades might need to spend time in a hospital.

Curtis, though, said he's been a lifelong fan of football and especially the NFL. In 2005, he bought season tickets for the 51st time in his life. He said that while moving around in the Air Force, he held season tickets to Broncos games for seven years, and then for four years to Cowboys games before being transferred to Georgia.

"I guess once you become a fan, and I've been one for 50 years, you have such a close association with the players," he said. "Back in the days with [former players] Mike Kenn, [Jeff] Van Note, [Steve] Bartkowski, and [Tommy] Nobis ... I've even made a few road trips on the charter. When you make those kinds of associations, you're much closer to the team."

The first game Curtis attended was the start of a three-way marriage. He went to Atlanta's very first preseason game in 1966, a 9-7 exhibition loss to the Eagles.

"That was my first date with the woman I married," he said. "Betty Hay. She's 92 now. The first 20 years, she was there with me home and away. There's no doubt that during that period we lost a lot more than we won, and she'd only go back occasionally. Now, I've got five or six friends in Atlanta … and about 10 tickets on the 50-yard line on the visitor's sideline. I've got some friends I didn't know I had. Sometimes they pay me for them. Sometimes they'll buy me a beer or something."

Although his wife has missed games over the years, Curtis claims he's never missed one in either old Atlanta-Fulton County Stadium, or the Georgia Dome. He also said he's been to 18 Super Bowls—but he's come close to missing a game or two.

"In the mid-1970s, my wife and I and some in-laws went to Europe," Curtis said. "I planned my trip so I would get back and not miss a Falcons game at home. The plane was delayed coming out of London, and got to Hartsfield [International Airport in Atlanta] at about 11 or 11:15, and I was on the phone telling everybody that was supposed to go to the game with me that I was going to be at the game come hell or high water. I forgot that I didn't have my tickets. I had to wait about an hour before some friends from Macon brought my tickets to me."

## LOYALTY HAS REWARDS

Curtis has seen some great moments, met and developed relationships with many players and coaches, and ended up in the NFL's "Hall of Fans" in Canton, Ohio in 1999. "People like to tell me I'm the only part of the Falcons to get there yet," he said.

He's also seen plenty of lowlights.

"I still think we had the better team in that Super Bowl [against Denver, in January 1999]. There was a safety [Eugene Robinson] who got himself in trouble the night before the game [when he was arrested for solicitation]," Curtis said.

"That hurt us, ruined things. That's the player that I would say upset me the most of all of them. I can't remember his name. That win in Minnesota [in the 1999 NFC Championship Game] was the greatest, I'd say, and that loss to Dallas [in January 4, 1981] was the worst. We had them beat."

Sharing his opinions takes little effort for the aging devotee.

"Deion [Sanders] was an enigma if there was one. He always had his white limousine down there at the stadium," he said. "How Rankin let that go on, I don't know. He wouldn't talk to the media sometimes, but he'd come and talk to me for some reason. Tremendous athlete, but a head too big for his body. [Trading Brett] Favre goes down as the most stupid thing any coaches ever did. I used to Indian-wrestle Brett Favre at a little bar the players used to go to. It's like Glanville sold him for $100."

It won't surprise knowledgeable NFL fans to learn which city The Colonel thinks least highly of, either.

"The ugliest of them all was my game in Philadelphia for the [NFC] Championship [on January 23, 2005]," Curtis said. "Those people were so mean to me. I'm proud of my Falcons uniform, and I wear it. I go to the bathroom at halftime, and they're chanting, 'Asshole, asshole, asshole,' and pushing me around. I took my stocking cap off, and showed my old gray hair, and said, 'Look you old son of a bitch, I'm 87 years old, and if you don't leave me alone, we're both going to jail, because I'm going to hit you in the mouth.'"

That offered only a temporary reprieve.

"Just a little later, a guy nearby said, 'I'll give $50 to anybody who'll piss on that Falcon.' I left. That was the worse there's ever been. I don't know if I'll ever go back."

But the man is not likely to ever stop being a Falcons fan. He's been close to many team officials over the years, he even went out from time to time with late owner and team founder Rankin Smith.

"I still call the owner Mr. Blank now. I've met him several times. I haven't been able to get as close to him as I was the Smiths, but I'm very happy about the way he's running the team," The Colonel said. "Rankin Sr. was an egomaniac, God bless him.

"I was with him on one occasion down on Bourbon Street when he was throwing chairs off a balcony across from the old

Absinthe House. He was an insurance man, with a whole lot of money, and he didn't have any football savvy whatsoever.

"He did mellow afterwards. His health started to fail, and like all of us when that happens, you look back and wish you didn't do some of the things you did. He has a great deal of respect and love in my heart. As far as I'm concerned, the Falcons wouldn't be here without him, and I wouldn't be with the Falcons."

## DUNN DEAL

Long before running back Warrick Dunn signed with the team as an unrestricted free agent in 2002, Dunns were part of the Falcons family.

Tom and Diane Dunn of Peachtree City, about 15 or 20 miles south of Atlanta, have held season tickets since they moved to Atlanta in 1979.

"The highlight of those early years was, of course, 1980, and not just because of the great regular season the team played. Diane was pregnant with our oldest son but never missed a game," Tom said. "It was also the year that [The University of Georgia] won the National Championship. The gentleman who sat in front of us ... was the father of two UGA students. Before every game, he would pull the hidden flask from his boot, pour a round for all who wanted, then stand up on his seat, turn toward the crowd and bellow, 'How 'bout them Dawgs!'

"The other thing that sticks out in my mind from that year is the end of the playoff game against the Cowboys. And how many of us just sat there in dead silence long after the clock ran out, having seen 'Our Year' disappear."

Many Falcons fans know the Dunns, perhaps only by sight, for the renovated ambulance they drive to games. With images of linebackers Tommy Nobis and Jessie Tuggle on one side, and quarterbacks Steve Bartkowski and Michael Vick on the other, the "Fanbulance" is hard to miss. It's a tailgating staple.

"All of the lights, siren, etc.—still work," said the eldest Dunn. "We added a tracking satellite dish and 26-inch TV to the rear, along with a microwave, blender, etc. Our son, Matthew, did Falcons graphics for the outside. When we arrive in the parking lot, the siren is actually the Falcon screech over AC/DC's 'Hell's Bells.'"

When the Dunn's first son, Matthew, was born in May of 1981, Bartkowski's wife, who had given birth, was in a nearby room. "Steve was at the peak of his popularity at the time, so the hospital was besieged with people trying to see him," Tom Dunn said. "Finding that we were huge Falcons fans, Steve brought us a gift that began our sports [particularly Falcons] memorabilia collection."

Dunn said Matthew scored the first youth football touchdown in the Georgia Dome, catching a 65-yard pass at halftime of a game against the Eagles in 1994.

Matthew's younger brother, Christopher, joined players at training camp in 1996.

"We snuck a peek inside [a room] to see [players] playing a fighting game on their Play Station and getting their hair cut," Christopher said. "They invited us inside to join in. I ended up beating [former cornerback] Tim McKyer.

"Another funny story that comes to mind took place in either 1990 or '91. My brother Matt and I were hanging out … at Atlanta-Fulton County Stadium. Coach Jerry Glanville recognized us and came over to say hello. He said, 'You guys follow me everywhere. Are you going to follow me when they run me out of town on a rail?'"

Some fans see each other's children grow up through their meetings at games, and check the passage of life in general while at the Georgia Dome.

"One of my favorite, yet saddest memories is of Inge Casey, who was one of the founding members of the Birdwatchers [one of the two big fan clubs, in addition to the Falcons Fanatics]," Dunn said. "She was one of those fans who could never find anything negative to say about the Falcons. Inge, born in Germany, was one of the most fascinating people you could ever meet. Anyway, during the summer of 1998, she was diagnosed with terminal cancer.

"She told Diane that she would accept her fate if she could only ask for two things. The first was to see her first grandchild born, which we felt sure she would, as her daughter was several months pregnant. The second was to see her Falcons in the Super Bowl. As for the second request, I didn't hold out much hope. The Falcons were coming off a decent 1997 season under first-year Coach Dan Reeves, but had a long way to go. I was hoping, at best, for a playoff appearance.

"The fairy-tale season concluded, of course, with a trip to the game in Miami. With much help from the Falcons organization, and hospices in Inge's hometown of Augusta and Miami, we were able to get her to the game, along with a visit to the team hotel. She was also interviewed by several TV and print folks. She had a wonderful time, despite the game result, and told us she could 'go in peace now.' Inge passed away the following May."

## FAN SQUABBLE

As the Falcons were en route to the NFC championship in 1998, tight end O.J. Santiago broke out the "Dirty Bird Dance" to celebrate a pair of touchdowns in a 41-10 win over the Patriots in Foxboro, Massachusetts on November 8.

"After the Philadelphia game [September 13] an old guy in the stands pointed at me and said, 'Dirty Birds, baby,' and from then on I was saying it everywhere," Santiago said. "I took it into the locker room, and before long everybody was saying it."

Running back Jamal Anderson later took credit for creating the dance, which featured high-stepping and flapping of the arms as if they were wings—although he wasn't the first to unveil it in a game.

Within 10 days of the dance's debut, deep snapper Adam Schreiber and right guard Gene Williams tried to copyright the phrase "Dirty Birds" for sale on T-shirts and other items.

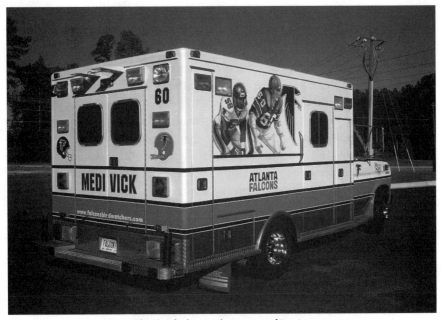

*The Fanbulance.* Photo courtesy of Tom Dunn

"Adam and I thought this was a pretty good thing, so we paid $250 to apply for a trademark for the term 'Dirty Birds Football,' and we hired an attorney to help form a corporation," Williams told the *Journal-Constitution*. "Basically, our mission is to get the Dirty Birds out there in the public."

A problem arose, however, because at roughly the same time, Alan Weiss, a 12-year season ticket holder and the manager of a local fish market, was trying to trademark the phrase, "DirtyBird" as well. He said he'd been hanging a "DirtyBird Zone," banner in the Georgia Dome on game days for three years. He'd already sold T-shirts and sweatshirts with the slogan.

There was some dispute over who applied first for the trademark, and some quibbling over the fact they had slightly different names in mind anyway.

"I think everybody can be happy," Weiss said. "I'm just one of the little people. I'm not out for blood. I don't see any reason we can't all get along."

In the locker room, Williams and Schreiber blasted a reporter who'd written about the situation in *The Atlanta Journal-Constitution*, chiefly because the story wrongly said Weiss was first to apply for trademark protection.

When the reporter explained that the story was written correctly, but edited to read incorrectly, the players didn't buy it. Schreiber, in particular, was livid, screaming at the reporter, the veins popping out of his neck, spit flying from his mouth.

Nearby, left tackle Bob Whitfield was getting a big kick out of the whole scene. "Hit him, Wink," he screamed at the reporter. "Come on, man, hit the dude."

Former Falcons general manager Harold Richardson eventually warned Williams and Schreiber to extract themselves from the disagreement with Weiss, suggesting there was little chance they could emerge without looking like two well-to-do pro athletes who were strong-arming the dreams of an everyday Joe trying to make an extra buck.

# CHAPTER FIFTEEN

# All the Way Up, and Down

There were few early indications that the hiring of Dan Reeves on January 21, 1997 would turn the Falcons around.

For one thing, he was a long-time advocate of power football (the running game), and he inherited a team that was stocked with players geared toward the run-and-gun, pass-happy offense of June Jones.

Some time after Jones was fired with a 19-29 record in three seasons—including 3-13 in 1996—owner Rankin Smith Sr. and president Taylor Smith went with their hearts in hiring Reeves, who'd been fired by the Giants.

Long criticized in the media for having an awkward front-office structure that lacked a general manager, the Smiths turned the keys over to Reeves. He was hired as the Falcons'

11th head coach and as the team's vice president of football operations. The Falcons now had a man with all the power.

"I'm in charge of football operations," he said the day he was hired. "I'm going to work with the people that are there. We'll see if we can work together. I have the ability to make the final decision. I had that for 12 years in Denver."

Soon a lot of heavy lifting took place, as the team retooled its roster in a dramatic way through free agency and a draft that after its early appearance as a flop, grew several players into key roles for the Super Bowl run of 1998.

First team officials re-signed free agent left defensive end Lester Archambeau, which was a bold move. Re-signing any defensive players from a unit that allowed an NFL all-time-worst of 4,751 passing yards in 1995 and registered just six interceptions in 1996 while allowing a whopping 461 points was not exactly a great public relations move.

But Archambeau, a Stanford graduate, was a spiritual leader of that defense—a wise man who had a bonding effect on a defensive line that featured end Chuck Smith and tackles Travis Hall and Shane Dronett. Next the team made a four-year, $13-million contract offer to transition free agent cornerback Ray Buchanan of the Colts. Indianapolis did not match it, and Buchanan joined the team.

Journeyman quarterback Chris Chandler, whom the Titans were moving out of the way so third-year star-in-training Steve McNair could take over, was acquired in a trade when Reeves and Co. chose him over free agent Elvis Grbac (49ers).

For a while, the Reeves regime was about anything but organization.

"We were going helter-skelter around here [for the first three months or so]," he said. "If I looked at everything on the whole, it would just blow you away."

One night, in the middle of a March storm, Reeves walked out of his room at the Falcon Inn—where he was living (wife Pam was in charge of moving from New Jersey)—and into his office. The power was out, and there was some sort of fuss down the hall.

"I was on the phone trying to get the deal done for [fullback Bob] Christian," said former general manager Harold Richardson, whose title at the time was assistant head coach for football operations. "I was working by candle, and I couldn't see, and Dan didn't know what all the hollering was."

Christian, waived by the Falcons in 1991 when he failed to make the team as a tailback after being drafted in the 12th round as a tailback, was signed as a free agent even though he missed the entire 1996 season with the Panthers because of a shoulder injury.

He took over for Craig "Ironhead" Heyward, whose contract could not be worked out, indicating the Falcons were going to make running back Jamal Anderson the centerpiece of their offense. That would be huge, and so was the role of Christian, who became one of the most underrated fullbacks of recent NFL vintage.

It didn't draw much attention at the time, but later in the spring, the Falcons signed free agent strong safety William White—previously of the Lions and Chiefs—to a two-year deal. He ended up being the glue of the secondary. Soon, starting safety Patrick Bates, who'd been charged with assault, was cut.

Eventual Super Bowl starter Dronett, whom the Falcons cut in 1996, was signed after the Lions cut him in 1997. "I didn't realize he was here, and [former defensive line coach] Bill [Kollar] had coached him and didn't like him," Reeves said.

## UP AND DOWN DRAFT

The draft did not sit well with Falcons fans as Atlanta traded the No. 3 overall pick to Seattle, where the Seahawks snagged a very good cornerback: Shawn Springs of Ohio State. The Falcons could've used Springs, but instead at No. 11—the Seahawks' original pick—they took Nebraska corner Michael Booker.

Reeves explained more than a year later that if former Tennessee quarterback Peyton Manning had elected to leave school after his junior season and go into the draft, the Falcons would've held onto the No. 3 pick to go after Manning.

Booker didn't end up a prize catch, yet early in the second round the Falcons selected overweight Indiana defensive tackle Nathan Davis, who ended up a far bigger booby-trap than Booker.

He even foretold his own demise, saying: "[Scouts] have been asking, 'Do you love the game?' Watching film of me from last season, it's not hard for me to see why they ask that."

The trade with Seattle brought the Falcons draft choices used on running back Byron Hanspard—whose career had a meteoric start before a knee injury slowed him—tight end O.J. Santiago, and strongside linebacker Henri Crockett. Seattle landed perennial Pro Bowl left tackle Walter Jones with another acquired pick.

Santiago (a third-round pick), Crockett (a fourth-round pick), and guard/center Calvin Collins—whom the team selected with a sixth-round pick that was acquired in a trade with Washington—all ended up starting in Super Bowl XXXIII. Booker played often in 1998 and started in place of injured right cornerback Ronnie Bradford in the NFC Championship Game win at Minnesota.

"I know people are going to say that they've heard all of this before, but it is different this time," perennial standout linebacker Jessie Tuggle told the *Journal-Constitution* that summer. "It's different now, because we have a respected head coach. He has a great staff that features former head coaches [offensive line coach and former Raiders coach Art Shell, and defensive coordinator and former Rams coach Rich Brooks]. The attitude of the players is tremendous, and that's about 80 to 90 percent of being successful right there."

Attitude did little good at first—the Falcons lost their first five games, and six of their first seven.

*Much-traveled quarterback Chris Chandler had one of the best seasons in franchise history while helping lead Atlanta to a 16-2 record and a Super Bowl berth in the 1998 season. His precision passes balanced a running attack powered by Jamal Anderson's franchise-record 1,846 rushing yards in 1998.*

# DEATH OF A PIONEER

For all the scorn directed at Rankin Smith Sr., much of it seemed hard to remember when he passed away on October 26, 1997. Done in by heart failure, he may have died with a broken heart.

The man who brought pro football to the Southeast, not to mention two Super Bowls to the Georgia Dome, passed away one season before his team made it to the NFL's grand ball. The Falcons fell to 1-7 the day of his death with a 21-12 loss at Carolina.

The Falcons had just seven winning seasons to their credit in 31 seasons when he died at age 72, but he was remembered widely for being a gentle man. He made some moves that were picked to shreds, but rarely for sake of ego. Rankin Smith Sr. simply wasn't a football man.

That wasn't a crime but an unfortunate reality.

He could've been a scourge had he accepted lucrative offers to move his team to Jacksonville early in the late 1980s. Instead, he stayed put, opting to keep his team at home in exchange for a new place to play, the Dome, although the state maintained ownership of the facility. "I could have made a killing in Jacksonville," he said once. "But this is home, and you do everything you can to stay home. I've always seen [relocation] as a last resort."

In an interview with *Journal-Constitution* columnist Terrence Moore shortly before his death, Smith acknowledged the ridicule:

"Sure, it hurts to hear those things. It would hurt anybody," he said. "But I'm the only non-moving target they can get to. So you have to expect it. I've been here [on the Atlanta pro sports scene] longer than anybody. There is only one cure to solving criticism, and that is winning."

## ON AN UPTICK

The Falcons began solving things after Smith's death, taking advantage of a new dynamic, a new kind of bond that had begun forming months earlier in the locker room. The Falcons were competing.

Suddenly, the offensive line jelled, Anderson got more comfortable, the defense improved, and Chandler began to click on the way to a passer rating of 95.1 that was second best in the NFL that season. Atlanta won six of its final eight games, narrowly losing on a late touchdown pass by quarterback Jake Plummer in the season finale at Arizona to finish 7-9 and just miss going .500 for the year.

"It's by far the best chemistry—10 times better than anywhere I've been," Chandler said while playing for the sixth of what would be eight NFL teams. "It seems like we stick together and do more things together. I just feel like guys care about one another more."

## A COUPLE MORE PIECES

There were two key acquisitions in 1998—and perhaps one subtraction. Free agent Eugene Robinson, a free safety who'd been with the Packers, signed with the team, and the Chargers called to offer wide receiver Tony Martin in a trade. Each man brought Super Bowl experience.

Robinson led a secondary that registered 19 interceptions in the 1998 season, and the speedy Martin (1,181) and fellow starting wide receiver Terrance Mathis (1,136) combined for just seven fewer receiving yards than the league's top tandem, Cris Carter and rookie Randy Moss of the Vikings. Martin was an outstanding replacement for wide receiver Bert Emanuel, a free-agent loss.

First, though, the Falcons bade farewell to enigmatic defensive tackle Nathan Davis, who lasted just eight minutes into practice on the second day of training camp. He simply walked away before his second pro season began.

"I've talked to him so many times, it doesn't make any difference," Reeves said after practice. "When he said he just didn't have it, and he didn't feel like he wanted to play, I didn't want the door to hit him in the back on his way out."

Davis said he was done in by taking diuretics two nights earlier while trying to reach the weight assigned to him before training camp. "I wasn't feeling it, and at this level you can't play that way," he told the *Journal-Constitution*. "The past two days I went 180 degrees from where I was the night before camp started. I was feeling good, in better shape, feeling strong.

"But I [lost] 13 pounds that night ... taking Vivarin [an over-the-counter stimulant], a lot of them. That didn't work too well."

Davis had appeared in just two games as a rookie. The Falcons waived him when he attempted to return a few days later.

"It hurts when you have a second-round draft choice you're hoping is going to be a player," Reeves said. "We tried everything we could to make him a player, but it's got to come from inside. You can't change a man's heart. He's probably the reason that we're doing some of the psychological testing we're doing now [for potential draft choices]."

# JAM SESSION

There were many reasons the Falcons were so good in 1998. The defense improved dramatically, finishing No. 2 in the league against the run, and with a great propensity for not only getting takeaways (44), but also scoring off them.

The defense scored five times that season, including a fumble return against the 49ers by middle linebacker Jessie Tuggle. That was the fifth of his career—an NFL record still intact as the 2005 season began. Defensive end Chuck Smith had 12 sacks.

Chandler had his best season—completing 58.1 percent of his passes for a whopping average of 9.65 yards per attempt (a

mark of 7.0 is solid in the NFL), 25 touchdowns, 12 interceptions, and a career-best passer rating of 100.9 that is still a franchise mark.

However, Jamal Anderson clearly was the locomotive.

The stocky fifth-year running back, a former seventh-round
draft pick from Utah (the 24th running back selected that year)
who had the confidence of a first-rounder, was unstoppable at
times while rushing an NFL-record 410 times for a franchise-
record 1,846 yards and 14 touchdowns.

Anderson arrived in the NFL in 1994 with an interesting
passport, having grown up in Newark, New Jersey, and then Los
Angeles, with a father, James, who was a security guard over the
years for, among others, singer Donna Summer, Muhammad
Ali, and Mike Tyson.

He was not impressed by celebrity—he expected it for himself. Boxer Sugar Ray Leonard, after all, was a family friend.

"My mom says when I was three or four years old, I used to
watch the old NFL films," Anderson said in 1998. "From
watching all those films and being around all those celebrities, I
learned that if you're going to play, you've got to be the best.
Always be No. 1—win, win, win. The competition among my
[four] brothers and [three] sisters was fierce. I remember they
said, '[Sugar] Ray is coming to your [Pop Warner football]
game,' and I was like, 'Cool. I'll have to score a couple touchdowns.' And then when I didn't score a touchdown, I cried. We
won, but I was furious I didn't score.

"Whether it's school, sports, speeches, whatever, I want
everybody to come away thinking, 'He's good.' If I'm giving a
commencement address at a high school, I want people to walk
away saying, 'He must do this for a living.' That's how I
approach everything."

After a 28-3 loss to the Jets in New Jersey, a game which
Chandler missed with an injury while 44-year-old quarterback
Steve DeBerg made his first (and last) start after coming out of
a five-year retirement (and a stint as Reeves's quarterbacks coach
with the Giants), the Falcons did some steamrolling.

They won their final eight regular-season games to win the NFC West—their second division title—beat the 49ers 20-18 in the Dome, and then upset the Vikings 30-27 in overtime in the NFC Championship Game.

Super Bowl XXXIII was not so warm and fuzzy. Atlanta was completely out of sorts, whether the indiscretions of free safety Eugene Robinson the previous evening had anything to do with it or not. Denver dominated on the way to a 34-19 win that made repeat champions of the Broncos on Janurary 31, 1999.

It was the last game of Denver quarterback John Elway's Hall of Fame career (he pushed DeBerg out of a job with the Broncos in 1983). He beat his first NFL head coach, Reeves, before retiring. He completed 18-for-29 for 336 yards and a touchdown, and ran for a score.

Robinson was beaten by Broncos wide receiver Rod Smith on an 80-yard touchdown. "Eugene left-center field," Elway said. "Rod got behind him."

After the game, the Falcons' free safety read a statement prepared with the help of his attorney. It was an especially awkward moment since, one day earlier, the Athletes in Action—a Christian organization—gave Robinson the Bart Starr Award, which honors one NFL player each year for exhibiting high moral character.

"I regret that ... I did not meet the high standards I have set for myself," Robinson said. "Let me reiterate ... I will be found innocent, although not righteous. I want to apologize to everybody ... but especially my wife. I love her very dearly, and I love my family very dearly. I know a lot of people will say this just sounds like another hypocritical Christian."

## GOING THE OTHER DIRECTION

I f opposites attract, the Falcons are proof. One season is rarely like the next, at least if the first one is good. Never in their first 39 seasons did they put back-to-back winning seasons together. It seemed like that streak would end in 1999.

It wasn't even close.

Within a month of the end of the 1998 season, the team cut wide receiver Tony Martin because he refused to delay a $400,000 roster bonus owed him while team officials awaited resolution of federal money laundering charges against him.

Martin's replacement, veteran former Giants wide-out Chris Calloway, was a disaster that season—fullback Bob Christian ended up the team's second-leading receiver, catching a career-high 40 passes (Mathis had 81 receptions). Calloway caught just 22.

Also, rookie wide receivers Eugene Baker and Rondel Menendez were part of a staggering and perpetual failure to draft receivers well—joining Jammi German and Tim Dwight of the 1998 draft, Mareno Philyaw in 2000, Vinny Sutherland and Quentin McCord in 2001, Kahlil Hill and Michael Coleman in 2002, and Jon Olinger and LaTarence Dunbar in 2003.

Weak-side linebacker Cornelius Bennett was cut in the off-season to free cap room for Keith Brooking, the team's first-round pick in 1998.

Team officials decided not to re-sign strong safety William White.

Anderson also boycotted the first 14 days of training camp in 1999, holding out until he got a better contract. Shortly after agreeing to a five-year, $32 million contract with a $7.5 million signing bonus, he said: "Believe me; I'm happy. We'll have the new dance so everybody will be smiling. It'll be the, 'Y2K Dirty Bird.' I won't have any problem. I'm like Baryshnikov, a natural."

That may have been a jinx, as Anderson would do very little dancing in 1999—and the Falcons followed up their 1998 ballet with a lead-footed clunker.

Chandler was hurt often that season, the offensive line—which did not have a starter miss a game in 1998—was hit with injuries and line coach Art Shell's surprise decision to replace left guard Calvin Collins with Bob Hallen between the preseason finale and the regular-season opener.

The final straw came in just the second game of the season—a Monday night at Dallas—when Anderson blew out the ACL in his left knee. He was untouched on the play, yet finished for the year.

Atlanta lost 24-7 with weak-armed quarterback Danny Kanell, the second of four straight losses to begin the season. Third-year pro Tony Graziani, who later went on to achieve greatness for the Los Angeles Avengers of the Arena Football League, did no better.

Ken Oxendine and a gimpy-kneed Hanspard, Anderson's chief replacements, averaged 3.2 and 2.8 yards per carry, respectively.

The Falcons finished 5-11, and after the season, Reeves said he underestimated almost a year earlier the value of the leadership provided by Bennett and White. Beyond their absence, Robinson—who finished out his two-year contract in 1999 after accepting a pay cut—no longer commanded as much respect among teammates.

By the last year of the century, the Falcons were missing almost all their tail feathers.

## GREASING THE SKIDS

The next season was worse, and it came with an omen as well.

Booker vanished from training camp one afternoon at Furman University, where special-teams coach Joe DeCamillis called him to participate in a punt team drill. "They came up to me, 'Where's Booker?'" said fellow cornerback Buchanan. "I looked up and said, 'Where is Booker?'"

Not even Booker's father, Michael Sr., knew where his son was—and he was at camp at his son's invitation. The player's wife was even in the dark for a while.

That night, young *Journal-Constitution* sportswriter Ken Sugiura, helping cover the NFL for the first time, went to get some grub at a Waffle House in tiny Travelers Rest, South

Carolina—just north of Furman—and there was Booker. He told Sugiura that he was planning to return to camp but declined further comment.

"I think he was having an over-easy [egg] and hash browns," Sugiura later told colleagues. "Probably tired of all those free ice cream bars at camp."

Actually, Booker was sick of football. "He said he wasn't sure if football was what he wanted to do," Reeves said of a late-night conversation with the cornerback.

Booker called Reeves again the next morning, told him he hadn't changed his mind, and headed back to Atlanta in his car while the team practiced.

"The further I got away from the training facility, it seemed like the more I wanted to be here," he told the *Journal-Constitution*. "When I got home, I took a shower, and laid down and thought about the situation. I called Dan [shortly before the afternoon practice], and I was just hoping he would accept me back."

Soon Booker was back with the team.

He'd explained that, after the morning practice two days earlier, well aware that he was in a battle for a roster spot, he found himself wrestling demons before opting to disappear.

"I came to [afternoon] practice, went to my locker, and I was just beating myself up," he said. "I don't want to get too spiritual, but the devil was working hard on me. It was like he was in my ear."

A couple weeks later, Booker was cut, going on to spend time with the Titans before his career ended.

## JAM'S BACK, TEAM'S STILL GONE

Anderson returned in 2000, and rushed for 1,024 yards, but the offensive line was dreadful, and while Chandler wasn't injured as often as 1999, he still found few targets. Atlanta went 4-12.

Chandler was not thrilled the following April, when quarterback Michael Vick out of Virginia Tech was made the No. 1

overall pick of the 2001 draft. Chandler kept the starting job but grew irritated again when Reeves made a point early in the 2001 season of playing his rookie quarterback a little in each game—a practice that eventually waned.

Anderson blew out the ACL in his other knee in the third game—a 34-14 win—but undrafted rookie free agent running back Maurice Smith of North Carolina A&T stole the show.

Atlanta was 6-4, but the running game bogged down when Smith played the last month and a half with a bad knee. The Falcons lost five of their final six games.

Arthur Blank finally, after considerable pushing, convinced Taylor Smith to sell the team in early December, closing the $545 million deal early in February of 2002.

Soon running back Warrick Dunn was signed as a free agent. A month later, Reeves—in the final days before the draft—changed the team's plans to select a wide receiver in the first round. Instead, big runner T.J. Duckett of Michigan State was selected, spelling the end for Anderson—he never played again after being cut in June.

Vick became the full-time starter in 2002, and the Falcons used an eight-game unbeaten streak in the middle of the season to finish 9-6-1. They then staged a stunning upset in the play-offs, becoming the first visiting team in 12 tries to win a post-season game in Lambeau Field. The 27-7 victory was the next-to-last bonafide high point of Reeves's coaching career, as the Falcons lost 20-6 at Philadelphia a week later.

## DEATH SPIRAL

In an August, 2003 preseason game at the Georgia Dome against the Ravens, Vick broke his right fibula near the ankle. Afterward, he and Blank were crying in the bowels of the Dome.

"It's like one of your children. He's 23 years old, and it's painful seeing how hard he's worked to get himself to this point," Blank said. "He'll play this year and lead this team, but it's just so hard to see that [happen] to somebody you care so much about."

Vick missed the team's first 11 games and came off the bench in the 12th—an absence that lasted roughly twice as long as original predictions. He could not prevent a loss at Houston as the dropped the team to 2-10.

It was a dreadful season. From Vick's injury, to the October suspension of cornerback Tyrone Williams for "conduct detrimental to the team"—which Reeves said was the first player suspension of his career—to distractions on and off the field, the vibe around team headquarters was mangled.

The Falcons rallied to win their opener at Dallas only to lose seven straight in a variety of fashions. The only other win without Vick came on the road, 27-7 over the Giants to give Reeves the 200th win over his coaching career.

Low points littered the autumn like leaves. Blank sent a letter of apology to ABC officials after his team lost 36-0 at St. Louis in a Monday night game. He also paid to run a letter of apology to fans in the *Journal-Constitution*. A halftime performance in the Georgia Dome by a local rap band degenerated into a mess, as the half-dressed 300-pound men of "Bonecrusher" sang lyrics laced with profane words and suggestions of murder that made the owner cringe.

Matters were never more tense than on October 29, when Reeves commented in a press conference that Vick—who was several weeks past his predicted return date—probably just needed to get out on the practice field, test it, and tough it out.

Asked simply what needed to happen to motivate his team, part of Reeves's answer was: "Mike needs to get back as soon as he possibly can. He talks about how he shouldn't come back [until he feels 100 percent], but ... he's not getting any better sitting on the sidelines."

Within minutes of Reeves's comments—this included mention that the quarterback would be working in drills that day—reporters gathered around his locker to ask if he was doing drills, if he was on the verge of returning. The third-year pro had no idea what reporters were talking about.

"That's the way Coach Reeves feels," he said. "The way I play is a little different, and we all know that. We all know that I rely on my legs as well as my arm. We all know that's the key to me, that's the key to my game. I need my wheels. I need this. This has to be 100 percent. I don't care what anybody says. It's my decision. Nobody can pressure me to make a decision. You say I need to get out there and practice, but I'm not going to jeopardize myself. If I go out there and try to play, and I'm 80 percent, I won't be able to focus and play the way I want. I did it in college. Every time I had an ankle injury I came back [early] and … I hurt it again. I know what that feeling is like, and I don't want it again."

Rarely did Reeves lose public composure as a head coach, excluding his sideline demeanor. The next day, though, he popped upon reading various news accounts.

"Nowhere in there did I indicate anything about getting [Vick] on the field," Reeves said angrily. "The drills I was talking about were with [trainer] Ron Medlin … doing football-related drills."

Within days, it was as if the volcano had spewed forth. Anxiety ebbed. The Falcons were officially feckless, and that was that. Vick didn't return for two more weeks, but there was a feeling that matters couldn't worsen after the Falcons lost a halftime lead to the Titans on November 23.

Dunn's season ended that day, as he tore a tiny ligament in his left foot in a 38-31 loss that left the Falcons 0-6 in games they led at halftime—as remarkable a statistic as this team put up in years.

For the next couple weeks, the Falcons were like crew and passengers on a doomed ship; they knew they couldn't avoid the iceberg ahead, so why sweat it?

Vick's first start was grand, a 20-14 overtime win on ESPN's *Sunday Night Football* on December 7, when defensive back Kevin Mathis returned an interception for the game-winning score. The quarterback was a bit rusty as a passer, completing just 16 of 33 passes for 179 yards with one interception.

But one could see why he's one of the most famous players in league history as he rushed 14 times for 141 yards and a score—the third highest rushing total by an quarterback in NFL history.

That was it for Reeves. Blank fired him two days later, saying that he was honoring Reeves's long-standing request that, if the owner had a career change in mind for him, he would let him know directly before the news came through the NFL's occasionally nefarious grapevine.

Blank was researching candidates to succeed Reeves and knew word would reach the coach eventually.

"There are no secrets in the NFL," the owner said. "We want to start the due diligence process for selecting a new head coach, following league policies, and we want to avoid unnecessary rumors, time drains and internal distractions as we do it."

The owner asked Reeves to finish out the season; but Reeves declined, leaving with an Atlanta mark of 52-61-1 in nearly seven seasons. Defensive coordinator Wade Phillips, who was leading the NFL's worst-ranked defense, took over on an interim basis. After getting whacked 38-7 the next week at Indianapolis, he managed wins at Tampa—eliminating the defending Super Bowl champions from playoff contention—and versus Jacksonville.

The 5-11 Falcons were in the dark—but a young, new light was around the corner.

# CHAPTER SIXTEEN

# Extra Points

It's quite probable nobody, other than his mother perhaps, has accused Patrick Kerney of being normal, and the odds on Janet Kerney saying such a thing might be long, too. When the Falcons made Kerney their first-round pick in 1999, they had high aspirations for him. They probably had no idea that he'd seem so often like he was actually high, too.

The former lacrosse star actually achieved considerable acclaim at the University for once attending a concert in nothing but a Speedo bathing suit. "That one certainly stuck out in the family Hall of Fame of disbelief," his mother told the *Journal-Constitution*.

At least he had something on that day. "Ask him about the party he went to in college wearing nothing but a bow tie, socks and shoes," said former nose tackle Ed Jasper.

"Had my checkered vans on, no socks, just shoes, bow tie, and after that I plead the fifth [amendment]," Kerney said.

Kerney, who went to his first Pro Bowl after the 2004 season—in which he registered a career-high 13 sacks to tie John Zook for third in Falcons history with 47 overall (trailing Claude Humprhey's 94.5 and Chuck Smith's 58.5)—will probably never land on a best-dressed list.

But costumes? Hey, he's probably cornered the market. He'd begged during the annual Christmas gift exchange for a teammate to get him a gorilla suit (he's notorious despite a multimillion dollar salary for being cheap; he still drives the 1996 Ford Bronco his parents gave him in college—although he did pay to have it painted in 2004).

Only late in 2003 did it finally happen.

"For years, there's been this defensive line fine board. The money gets pooled, and at the end of the year, we split it up and go buy each other a present," he said. "Basically, you tell the guy getting your gift what you want. For years, I'd been saying I want a gorilla costume and a banana costume, or a bear costume and a honeybee costume.

"Fish [Jasper] would draw my name, and say, 'I'm not getting a grown man a gorilla suit.' Well, finally, a rookie, Demetrin Veal, drew my name, and I said, 'You've got no say in this. You're getting me a gorilla suit.'"

Why a gorilla suit?

"Think about this: you're on a beach reading a book, having a great vacation, and all of a sudden you hear screaming, 'Oh my gosh, help me, help me,' and you see a banana running down the beach," Kerney said. "You say, 'That's weird.' And you go back to your book. Seconds later, you hear, 'Get back here you bastard!' and there's a gorilla chasing it. That would make your vacation. It could rain the rest of the week, you could get dumped by your girlfriend, and it would still have been a great vacation if you saw that."

Kerney tested the first part of his gag out one spring day in 2004, racing down a Charleston, South Carolina beach dressed like an ape.

Soon after that, he was able to go the whole nine yards, as long as he can find a willing partner. He scored a banana costume for Christmas in 2004.

# READY...WRESTLE!

It's doubtful that any Atlanta player suffered more than former guard/tackle Bill Fralic, inasmuch as he was a four-time Pro Bowl player while with the Falcons from 1985-1992, when the team went a combined 44-84-1, including the team's one playoff appearance in that span. Talk about laboring in obscurity ... .

The former Pitt star held out twice, and considered forgoing football altogether after the Falcons made him the No. 2 overall pick of the 1985 draft. He was going to be a pro wrestler—Bill "The Bull" Fralic—when he didn't like the tenor of contract negotiations.

"I named that sucker 'Bull' myself when he was seven years old," his father, Bill Sr., told *The Atlanta Journal*. "Billy is going to be earning a living real shortly. I sure as hell hope it's with the Atlanta Falcons, but if it isn't, we can't wait for a year or so to go by to take a shot at negotiating with them again. He has to do something in the meantime.

"I don't make that much money," said the elder Fralic, at the time a Pittsburgh steelworker, "and Billy's gotten used to living a little high on the hog. I know he doesn't want to come back down to living on the allowance I give him.

"All I know is what when Billy makes up his mind to do something, he does it. We didn't just pull that figure out of a hat. I know what Billy expects to get and he can't see why anybody [in the draft] should make more than him. Whatever happens, Billy's not going to be caught with his pants down."

Fralic was soon wearing Falcons pants and earning a slew of honors as one of the great blockers of the past quarter century—good enough to earn consideration for the NFL Hall of Fame, something that may have eluded him because he played most of his career with Atlanta.

# BACK UP, BUDDY...

After allowing 385 points for the second straight season in 1994, the first as head coach for June Jones, Falcons officials decided they desperately needed an impact linebacker—so they signed free agent Darryl Talley.

He'd been great while playing for the Buffalo teams that went to four straight Super Bowls in the early 1990s. Talley, hated Atlanta though—he hated the system, and team officials didn't care for him, either. It was clear as the 1995 season wore on that he wouldn't be asked back in 1996.

So he showed up at the Georgia Dome for the season finale on Christmas Eve in 1995 with a U-Haul trailer hooked up to the back of his car. He was splitting as soon as the game was over—getting out of town for good.

It seemed a safe bet. The Falcons were playing the defending world-champion 49ers, who'd beaten Atlanta six of their seven previous meetings, including a 41-10 whipping earlier that season in San Francisco.

Alas, the Falcons knocked the 49ers out of the No. 1 seed in the NFC, winning 28-27. Not only would the Cowboys hold home-field advantage through the postseason (and go on to win their third Super Bowl in four seasons), but the Falcons earned a playoff spot with a 9-7 record.

# BURNT TO A CRISP

When Jim Mora put together his first staff as a head coach, he drew considerable praise from colleagues around the league when he landed one of the great offensive line coaches in history, Alex Gibbs.

Gibbs wasn't an easy grab (the Texans and Giants were known to pursue him), and he wasn't an easy keep. He stayed in the role for one year before moving into a consultant's role, much as he had four years earlier with the Broncos.

After working like a madman on Denver coach Mike Shanahan's staff, Gibbs became a part-time coach during the

2001-2003 seasons, spending half of each week at his Phoenix home, and half with the Broncos.

Eventually, he longed to make a bigger impact, and Mora, with whom Gibbs worked in San Diego years earlier, came calling. Arthur Blank played a big role—making Gibbs the game's highest-paid offensive line coach.

Shortly after he was hired, in Atlanta Gibbs explained his burnout in Denver. "I was in a state of exhaustion, a state of depression, there's no question about it," he said. "I knew I had to do something. I was so mad at me and everybody else. I didn't give a damn about anything. I was that disoriented.

"I had burned myself to a frazzle. I couldn't keep going. People outside of coaching can't understand. You're working 117-hour weeks, six or seven months a year, with no days off—nothing."

Gibbs spoke to members of the media perhaps a couple times in training camp and very early in the season of 2004, and then went into his more standard boycott of the ink, opting not to comment for publication the rest of the season.

He stayed mad, though. He was often in flames on the sidelines during games. When Mora was asked about it, he said, "Oh, that's just Alex."

After Gibbs's son, David, was fired by Shanahan at midseason in 2004 as the Broncos' secondary coach, the elder Gibbs spoke via phone several times with a Denver reporter, who first reached him at his Falcons office at about 4 a.m. one morning.

A few days later, Gibbs barked at the reporter, "When are you going to write the story? What are you waiting on?"

"What is the story? You haven't told me what's going on." The reporter asked.

"Ahhh, you're just another one of Shanahan's guys." Gibbs shot back.

Soon after the season, Gibbs was planning to commute during the season from Phoenix, again as a consultant—this time with the Falcons.

# SWEET DREAMS

As the Falcons neared the end of training camp in 2004, they knew it would be their last at Furman University. Owner Arthur Blank was building dormitories near the team facility back in Flowery Branch, Georgia to hold future camps.

Things became goofier than normal—several players admitting to having strange dreams.

"There was a dream about me buying a dog from [defensive tackle Chad] Lavalais, and it's always crapping like a bird," said right guard Kynan Forney. "I'm always cleaning up after it, and Lavalais's mom keeps screaming at me because I won't eat the food."

Even former director of communications Aaron Salkin told *The Atlanta Journal-Constitution*, "I had a dream about leeches coming down the walls in my room. I called security, and they wouldn't do anything about it. I equated the leeches with the media."

One just knows that Kerney was in on this.

"The Harveys were the family across the cornfield from me growing up. In this dream I'm in a back room of their house, and these mafia guys are saying it's a death sentence for me," he said. "So I haul ass out of there because I don't want to get the dirt nap. All of the sudden I go, 'Keys,' and some valet kid chucks me keys to a Range Rover. Then I'm at my first high school, running up a hill to the hockey rink, and I see a navy blue Range Rover up there that must be mine.

"There's 15 mafia dudes chasing me, and I'm thinking I can out-leg these boys. These guys are like 60 years old, and they're running me down! I'm fumbling the keys, and I turn, lock one out [a pass-rushing technique], shed the block, head back down hill and wake up."

That's not all.

"I had another one," Kerney said, "where I'm on Mt. Airy Road, near the farm where I grew up. What was I driving? A giant ice cream sandwich. All of a sudden, I see a cop, and I say, 'Ooh, I better turn on my lights. I better stop swerving. Wait a second. They're going to pull me over. I'm driving an ice cream sandwich.'"

## GET HIM SOME BABES

Former running back Harmon Wages, who became a sports-caster in Atlanta, quickly earned a reputation as a playboy while playing mostly as a reserve from 1968-1971 and in 1973. Because he wore No. 5 and had fair hair, he was on more than one occasion compared with Green Bay running back Paul Hornung, who also wore No. 5.

One time, after Wages rushed 10 times for 71 yards in a game, coach Norm Van Brocklin demonstrated that he wasn't a full-time curmudgeon. "Somebody said he was like Paul Hornung," Van Brocklin said. "If he'll have a career like Hornung, I'll toss in a few Playboy clubs."

## HOLDING DOWN THE FORT

Former linebacker Tommy Nobis and equipment manager Horace Daniel spent all but one of the Falcons' first 40 years working for the team (Nobis spent a year in the private sector after his playing career ended and before joining the front office, and Daniel joined the team in its second season, 1967).

Yet former center Jeff Van Note saw the most—at least from the trenches.

Drafted in the 11th round as a defensive lineman in 1969, the former Kentucky star still credits Van Brocklin for his career, which lasted all the way to 1986. "He switched me to center, and I sure wouldn't have been around long if he didn't," said Van Note, who's spent many seasons on the Falcons' broadcast team.

Van Note's 18 years of service were not only most in team history (one more than former tackle-turned-local-politician Mike Kenn), but also tied for third most in NFL history with one team. Only Rams offensive tackle Jackie Slater and

Redskins cornerback Darrell Green (20 seasons each), and Vikings defensive end Jim Marshall (19) did more time.

He and former defensive end Claude Humphrey share the Falcons record of six Pro Bowl appearances while playing for Atlanta. That's one more than linebacker Jessie Tuggle, Kenn, and Nobis.

## LOOK OUT FOR THAT GUY

When coach Leeman Bennett cut former free agent defensive end Greg Fields in 1982, Fields refused to leave his hotel room. Allegedly in possession of a gun, he was escorted out by Suwanee police.

"He said he was going to come back and kill people," Van Note said.

Fields went to the USFL's Los Angeles Express in 1983. When he was cut there, he slugged coach John Hadl.

## GIVING BACK OVER AND OVER

Warrick Dunn made it to the Super Bowl in February 2005, but not as a player. He left the Tampa Bay Buccaneers and signed with the Falcons in the spring of 2002 only to watch the Bucs win the world championship that very year. The Falcons' loss to the Eagles in the 2005 NFC Championship Game was as close as he's gotten while in an Atlanta uniform. However, Arthur Blank always seems to be talking about winning in the "Super Bowl" of life, and Dunn's a repeat champion there.

The Falcons' smallish running back likely qualifies as the team's most giving player, at least when it comes to charitable works, and that's saying something for perhaps the NFL's most philanthropic team.

Blank, whose family foundation awards tens of millions of dollars in grants and donations each year, pushes every member of his organization to get involved in charity, not that Dunn needs the nudge.

Long before he moved to Atlanta, he started the "Homes for the Holidays" program in Tampa and his native Baton Rouge. Each year, around Thanksgiving, he makes a down payment on homes for single mothers and their families, and with the help of corporate sponsors, he helps furnish the homes.

He's been featured on numerous TV shows, in *People* magazine, and a few days before Super Bowl XXXIX in Jacksonville, he was honored by the NFL as winner of the Walter Payton NFL Man of the Year in 2005. Since 1997, his program has helped 52 mothers and 135 children and dependents move into homes.

Dunn started the program in honor of his mother, Betty Smothers, who was killed as an off-duty police officer while working a security detail when Dunn was in high school. Dunn's mother, who died in 1993, dreamed of owning her own home and worked a second job to try to make it happen.

"She was really everything to me," said Dunn, who after his mother's death played a huge role in helping raise his five younger siblings. "She taught me a lot about life."

NFL players such as Arizona Cardinals quarterback Kurt Warner and Kansas City Chiefs kick-return phenomenon Dante Hall have adopted similar programs in their teams' cities and hometowns.

Blank glows when talking about not only Dunn's charitable works, but also those of many players.

Statistics show the Falcons lead the NFL in contributions to their community, most of it to benefit children, according to a *Journal-Constitution* story during the 2004 season.

The team led the league in money given to charity (more than $2 million in 2004), player appearances for charities (about 700), and nonprofit foundations started by athletes and coaches (eight). The Falcons also have the largest staff devoted to community work (seven full-time employees).

"The more people who like you in the community, the better chance you have of staying on the team," said fullback Justin

Griffith, exercising with kids at a Boys and Girls Club in southeast Atlanta. "If you can be well known in the community, a lot of good things can happen for you."

Blank's dedication to charity mirrors much of the work of Coca-Cola pioneer Robert Woodruff, whose donations helped many Atlantans and local institutions in the 20th century.

"I'd like to be remembered as one of the best at setting a good example," Blank told the *Journal-Constitution*. "Not just in the NFL, but of owners of hockey, baseball, basketball teams and other organizations—on and off the field."

Dunn has gone out of his way to become an ambassador of this ideal.

In 2004, he traveled with teammate Keith Brooking and Ravens tight end Todd Heap to visit U.S. Troops in Europe. In 2005, he again went overseas; visiting Kuwait, Afghanistan, and Iraq with Patriots special teams ace Larry Izzo on behalf of the NFL.

"I got to experience some things," Dunn said. "You go to Afghanistan, and it's the sixth poorest country in the world. I go to Iraq, and I see how those people are living on the front lines, how it's like they are in prison and free at the same time. There are barricades everywhere and just the tension that is everywhere. And you can hear the car bombs and shooting. This thing is way intense."

In Baghdad, Dunn got an up-close sense of what troops were experiencing daily. He spoke of the experience in a story on the team's web site.

"I can understand why people would be scared. You hear bombs. There are car bombs going off. Those are live rounds being fired. It's no joke," he said. "If a person goes, their life will be in jeopardy. Period. We're just fortunate enough that nothing happened. We were flying in choppers and somebody could have fired a missile at the chopper.

"Someone could have had a car bomb and rammed into our checkpoint. Someone could have shot a missile into one of the buildings we were in. What's weird about this thing is, a couple of camps we visited the night before they were hit. That's crazy. That's surreal."

Dunn had a message for soldiers.

"I know one thing I remember saying is that, 'Even though I may be on television and a lot of people may know who I am, the true heroes are you guys because you guys are on the front lines. You guys are fighting, making sure that we're able to get up every day and not worry, and America thanks you for that,'" he said. "'And I know the NFL, the players, the Atlanta Falcons—we thank you for that. You guys give us freedom.'"

# CHAPTER SEVENTEEN

# Aiming Higher

The Falcons hired Jim Mora as their new head coach on January 9, 2005—less than a month after Rich McKay was hired as the team's president/general manager.

Mora is the team's 13th head coach—13 may be lucky this time.

The son of the former Saints and Colts coach by the same name, Mora was relatively unknown to many Falcons fans, having previously spent seven years with the 49ers, five as defensive coordinator.

The former San Diego and New Orleans assistant made himself known quickly, setting down the law, calling for a quick pace at all times, in practice and in workouts, and lofty standards in all that players do relative to football. It paid off immediately.

Although the team did not have a huge off-season after the 5-11 season of 2004, at least in terms of the number of new front-line players added, the Falcons had a new attitude, and an unmistakable sense of urgency.

Fired by the Packers, defensive coordinator Ed Donatell was practically hired out of new (and old) Redskins coach Joe Gibbs's office once Mora got him on the phone. Mora also brought his friend Greg Knapp—the 49ers former offensive coordinator—and a couple other San Francisco coaches with him (linebackers tutor Chris Beake and secondary coach Brett Maxie).

Offensive line coach Alex Gibbs revamped the style of blockers, quarterback Michael Vick was healthy again, and the team scored a grand slam in signing free agent-former Raiders defensive tackle Rod Coleman (11.5 sacks in 13 games) and selecting 20-year-old Virginia Tech cornerback DeAngelo Hall in the first round.

Then the Birds took to the air. Atlanta won its first four games en route to a 9-2 record, and ran away with the NFC South title with an 11-5 record, resting key players in the final two games, which were losses.

Mora didn't register any press conference blowups on a par with the two or three that made his father famous, although he sparred with a few reporters. It was enough to develop a reputation for being curt when agitated.

"I've been in both situations," said former NFL and Falcons quarterback Hugh Millen, one of Mora's roommates at the University of Washington where Mora was a walk-on linebacker. "I've been asked the questions, and [as a Seattle broadcaster] asked the questions. I've known Jimmy more than half his life. My explanation is that Jimmy is the most loyal person I have ever known in any capacity. He's loyal, perhaps to a fault, where it could harm him down the line in his career if he's loyal to the wrong person."

Mora has said he can handle criticism, but not skepticism. Yet, he doesn't tolerate either without swallowing hard, and most journalists by their job descriptions are to cast a critical,

*Head coach Jim Mora and owner Arthur Blank*

even suspicious eye on their subject matter. Their employers demand as much.

Sometimes it seems that Mora takes criticism—or even third-party comments—as mean-spirited jabs or skepticism about him or his team. As Millen suggested, he's very defensive about his players and coaches, and admits as much.

No matter—he resonated with the players.

"Awesome," nose tackle Ed Jasper said. "His pregame motivation, man, he's jacked. You know when you look in somebody's eyes, and you can tell it's there? That's the way he is. We feed off it. You come out of the locker room … you're juiced."

Just 42 when hired, Mora had a knack for staying pumped, yet relating very well with fellow coaches, with players, and even media (most of the time).

"I talked to [long-time equipment manager] Horace [Daniel] and said, 'How's Jimmy doing?'" Millen said. "He said, 'Man, I can't tell you. He's the only guy who in all the years will set the table for you, have a meal with you, ask you how you're doing?' That's just how he does it. He doesn't do it with a grand scheme in mind, that's just how it is."

A meticulous note-taker who has saved decades of scribbling, tapes of his favorite players, and scores of books relating to football and motivational methods, including *The Art of War* by Sun-Tzu, Mora left a major impression in almost no time at all.

He's very good at mixing up his messages, keeping them fresh for players.

"It's like with your kids. If you get on them all the time, click! They turn it off," Mora told the *Journal-Constitution.* "It's like the old Charlie Brown [teacher going], 'Wah-wah-wah-wah.' They don't hear you. You have to be conscious of where you are during the season, what you said the week before, and try to keep it pretty even."

It worked in spades.

"Jim presents himself as one of the guys, and yet nobody challenges his head coach authority," former wide receiver Jimmy Farris said. "He's able to toe that fine line of being one of the guys while still maintaining that, 'Hey, I'm still the head coach.'

*Michael Vick and Jim Mora*

"It's a very fine line, but I think his years as a coordinator and dealing with guys on a personal level … you know, guys feel more comfortable coming to a coordinator or position coach than a head coach to talk about personal things. That helped him.

"When he's in the locker room, you don't look around and say, 'Hey, the head coach is here; watch what you say.' For a guy like him, it's easy to do because we feel like he's one of the guys leading us."

Thanks to an uncanny connection between coaches and players, Atlanta rode a vastly improved defense, outstanding special teams, and the league's No. 1 rushing attack, all the way to the NFC Championship Game at Philadelphia.

Along the way, Donatell preached: "The best player on our team is our team."

Special teams coordinator Joe DeCamillis—one of the last holdovers from Reeves's initial 1997 Atlanta staff (the other is strength and conditioning coach Al Miller, who like DeCamillis was with Reeves with the Broncos and Giants)—did his thing. Frequently, DeCamillis—a former college All-America wrestler—screams: "Let's get flat-ass rolling." Roll they did, sparking return ace Allen Rossum to his first Pro Bowl trip (as an alternate).

"He and [assistant strength and conditioning coach] Rocky [Colburn] come up with something every week to inspire guys and challenge them," said Dana DeCamillis, wife and muse to one of the league's top assistants of any ilk. "He always rehearses the speeches with our two daughters and me. It's awesome. He talks about Genghis Khan, Attila the Hun, anything to make it seem like a battle."

Ever veto a speech?

"No. Sometimes I laugh a little bit," Dana DeCamillis told the *Journal-Constitution*. "With the Genghis Khan deal, the girls said, 'Dad, putting someone's arm and leg in your trophy case. I don't know about that.' There was the one about the Berzerkers—a group of Vikings."

## ROLLING UP THE MOUNTAIN

The Falcons crushed the Rams 47-17 in a second-round playoff game, ending a Mora family postseason skid. His father was 0-6 in the playoffs with the Saints and Colts, something that drew his son's teases.

A 27-10 loss to the Eagles ended the season. But Falcons fans are optimistic about the future and planning to end one very horrible streak in 2005 by putting together the first back-to-back winning seasons in the franchise's 40 years.

The off-season signing of free agent middle linebacker Edgerton Hartwell, a Pro Bowl-caliber player previously with the Ravens, extended a run of local optimism.

It will be largely up to Mora to keep everybody on task, and it's not hard to find believers.

After the win over the Rams, Millen, Mora and two more college buddies—Mark Pattison and Wayne Hagen—tossed back a couple beers in the coach's Dome office with Mora's father and brothers. It was a rare relaxed moment for Mora, who charges forward at nearly all times.

They all believe Mora's the man in Atlanta.

"He's got a great staff, that's the Xs and Os part of it, and he's got ... something compelling about his personality that makes guys play hard for him," Millen said. "You can't read about that; you have it or you don't. He's a guy that in his own mind expects this of himself, and probably feels like he was born to be a football coach; it's in his DNA."

Outside the Dome that night, and around Atlanta long afterward, there were—and are—plenty of fans who agree. The Dome was sold out for every game in the first three seasons after Blank bought the team in 2002, and Blank said in 2005 there were tens of thousands of fans on a waiting list for season tickets.

Vick has a new nine-year contract, and the combination of Blank, McKay, and No. 7 has 'em ready to roll in Atlanta, not that they weren't there all along.

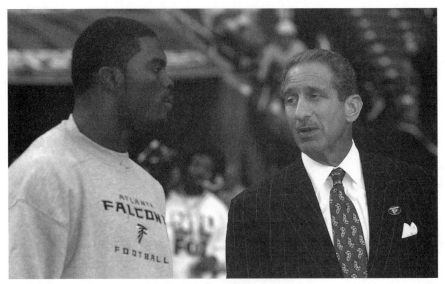

*Michael Vick and Arthur Blank*

After Falcons uber-fan Colonel Joe Curtis was beaten up in New Orleans back in 1999—when he said Saints fans were giving him a hard time about Reeves—he eventually explained what happened. "Coach Reeves told me, 'If you're the kind of fan who'll fight for me and the team, you're my kind of fan.'"

Those fans have been around for years. It's been a long time coming, and now they're out of hiding and ready to be heard consistently in the raucous Georgia Dome—as long as one requirement is met.

As Falcons founder Rankin Smith Sr. once said: "There is only one cure to criticism—and that is winning."

Winning time seems to have arrived.

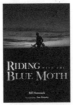

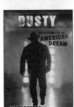